THE INNER LIFE

THE MYSTIC LIFE

THE INNER LIFE

Foundations of
Christian Mysticism

by
George H. Tavard

PAULIST PRESS
New York/Paramus/Toronto

Library of Congress
Catalog Card Number: 75-32858

ISBN: 0-8091-1927-7

Published by Paulist Press
Editorial Office: 1865 Broadway, N.Y., N.Y. 10023
Business Office: 400 Sette Drive, Paramus, N.J. 07652

Printed and bound in the
United States of America

Contents

Contents

To
George and Kitty Cole

Foreword

With the spread of the spiritual movement called, in various places, "spiritual renewal," "charismatic" and "pentecostal," the classical Christian Churches, including the Roman Catholic Church, are invited to recover the spiritual richness of their heritage. The "horizontalism" which has marked a good deal of theology since the Second World War seems on the wane with a progressive re-emphasis on the transcendence of God and his presence and action beyond reach of human plans and efforts. The current interest in esoteric mysticisms, borrowed, with considerable simplifications, from Asia, is also the sign of new times dawning for the religious dimension of modern life. The existence of the "Jesus movement" and the popularity of "Jesus" as a theme for songs and musicals point up the failure of pure secularism to establish itself as the meaning of modern times.

The present volume is intended to be an introduction to the mystical dimension of Christian, especially Catholic, life. I have attempted to give a traditional view of the elements that go into the making of the spiritual life in keeping with the basic beliefs of Christianity as interpreted and experienced by the great mystics. These elements are of two kinds: there is a structure or framework, and there are forces or powers which are at work within this

1

structure; altogether, the structure and these dynamic principles activate the inner life, which then develops according to a fairly common pattern. This explains the plan of this book: after a general introduction (Chapter 1), the structure of the inner life is described (Chapter 2), the dynamic principles are outlined (Chapter 3), and the development of prayer is examined (Chapter 4).

The bibliography is far from exhaustive. Its aim is only to provide interested readers with titles for collateral reading. Most of the volumes listed are recent, but I have added a number of classics, for nothing can replace first-hand acquaintance with the great masters of the spiritual life, in whatever century they may have lived.

I have systematically abstained from burdening my text with footnotes, although every line could be well documented. The reason is, of course, that this book has been conceived for wide use, not only by students who are concerned about scholarship, but also by readers, lay or clerical, who are simply seeking to deepen the dimension of their prayer and to enter more completely into their inner life.

George H. Tavard
Methodist Theological School
Delaware, Ohio

1
General Introduction

The inner or spiritual life is the life of the spirit in us, the life by which our human spirit aspires to union with the Spirit of God, and eventually attains to such a union. Our conception of the spiritual life will naturally vary with our concepts of the human spirit and the Spirit of God.

We may distinguish two basic concepts:

1. *Monistic.* The human spirit and the Spirit of God are not essentially different. Man is an emanation, an aspect or a manifestation of the divine principle, no matter what name is given to this principle. In this case, union with the divine Spirit will consist in entering the hidden depths of our own being, in which we are already one with God, even though our daily self-consciousness operates on such a superficial level that we are not commonly aware of our close identity with the divine.

This may be found, with many variations, in the oriental religions, especially Hinduism, Buddhism and Taoism, which are metaphysical religions. The idea underlies Confucianism, which is an ethical religion. It is also implied in the recent forms of oriental religiosity that have spread into some sections of Western society.

3

2. *Prophetic.* The human spirit and the Spirit of God are essentially different. God is the all-other, transcendent, unattainable. The prophetic faith is man's acceptance of and commitment to a transcendent God who, paradoxically, out of his mysterious and loving design, makes himself known to and through a prophet. Union with God consists essentially in obeying the revelation, in following the way taught by God's prophet. This does not rule out a union to God by love, but this union must express itself ethically as obedience. This is found in the prophetic religions: Judaism, Islam, Zoroastrianism.

There are also *mixed types:* animism, as still practiced in many parts of Africa, has a monistic basis; yet the way to discover our fundamental divine principle is mediated by prophetic personalities (Shaman, witch doctor, priest . . .). Most Western mythologies belong to this mixed type (Greek, Roman, Aztec, etc.). Our knowledge of primitive religion is sketchy; it may have been of any historically known type or of some unknown type.

The *incarnational* type is the unique feature of Christianity. The God who is transcendent, all-other, unattainable, has become one of mankind through the Incarnation. This shatters both monistic and prophetic assumptions, while it also justifies the basis of monism and prophetism: God is both immanent (tendency to monism) and transcendent (prophetism). Thus an incarnational spirituality fulfills both the desire for union with the immanent divine principle, and obedience to prophetic revelation.

Christian spirituality is founded on the New Testament. That is, its center is the Person of Christ, the God-Man, as he is known through the New Testament. Since he is the Word of God, the way of spiritual life consists in hearing and following him. Christian spiritual life requires familiarity with the New Testament. And since the New Testament can only be understood in the context of the Church who wrote it, it also requires acquaintance with the way in which the Church proclaims the New Testament, that is, with the liturgy or worship. In the liturgy, the Church announces the Word to the faithful, calling them to union with Christ. Such a union with Christ takes place in keeping with the theological realities which are implied in the revelation. The inner life therefore should be examined theologically. And since many authors have described their own spiritual life, in its beginnings, its ascent and its high points, Christian mysticism and the writings of the mystics should also be studied.

In the theological study of Christian spiritual life, many schools of thought and practice have developed. A word should be said about the main ones, so that the present work may be set in its proper context.

There are three main periods of spiritual theology:

1. *Patristic.* The spirituality of the Fathers is kerygmatic (stressing the Logos or Word, plus listening to the Word in obedience); sacramental (stressing the way of union with Christ through symbolic actions); anagogical (God is found in my soul, which is the image of heaven); unsystematic (there is no system or formula for union with God through Christ—rather it is reached through full participation in the Church's life).

2. *Medieval.* The spirituality of the Middle

Ages is essentially monastic (the monk is the ideal); scriptural (Holy Scripture is the basic revelation of spiritual life); meditative (meditation upon Scripture is the way to contemplation); contemplative (the mysteries of the Incarnation may be "seen" by the eyes of faith, and such a contemplation is the mainspring of union with Christ).

3. *Modern.* After the Middle Ages, and especially during the Counter-Reformation, spiritual authors began to apply the incipient science of psychology to their study of the inner life, thus elaborating systems of ascetical training destined to prepare for union with God. The main schools are the Ignatian (from St. Ignatius of Loyola) and the French school (17th century).

Religious orders are often marked by the spirituality of their founder or at least of the period in which they were established. The preaching and the spiritual direction provided by their members will often depend on some theological emphasis special to their origins. Thus we may distinguish:

● the spirituality of monastic families: Benedictines; Cistercians (some main authors in our century: Dom Lehodey, Thomas Merton); Carmelites (especially Discalced Carmelites: St. Teresa of Avila, St. John of the Cross, St. Thérèse of Lisieux); Carthusians (Vernon Moore);

● the spirituality of friars (established in the early 13th century): Dominicans, Franciscans (stress on cult of the humanity of Christ);

● the spirituality of most Congregations (founded since the 16th century) is dominated by the Society of Jesus, mainly because of the widespread influence of the *Exercises* of St. Ignatius; many are also influenced by the French School, more specifically through the Sulpicians (M. Ollier).

The present introduction to the inner life is based upon the following principles and plan. The spiritual life depends on a sacramental, liturgical and theological framework which will be called here its constitutive elements (Chapter 2). These elements are given life in us, in our personal participation in them, through subjective principles deriving from God's grace; these will be called the dynamic principles of spiritual life (Chapter 3). The union of these two dimensions should normally lead to a development of the inner life, manifested chiefly in changing patterns of prayer (Chapter 4).

This introduction does not follow any specific school of spirituality. It corresponds, of course, to my own theological orientation and spiritual experience, as documented in my previous volumes, especially in *The Church Tomorrow* (Herder and Herder, 1965) and *Meditation on the Word* (Paulist Press, 1968). It is naturally indebted to what I have learned from the writings and life of the founder of my Order, Emmanuel d'Alzon (1810-1880).

This essay differs from many in that it does not attempt to map out every development of the inner life. It does not try to present a system to be followed or a complete explanation of the ins and outs of spiritual progress. It is an outline, made with the purpose of assisting reflection on spiritual life rather than of telling people what they ought to do to develop their inner life. It is my conviction that the elements analyzed here are essential to all Christian spiritual experience and, within their frame-work, it is possible to develop freely one's interior life into all the main directions described by spiritual authors of the Christian tradition. This is therefore not written against any specific orientation, although it is to be expected that some will find my approach more congenial, especially if they have been nurtured in a Catholic context.

2
Constitutive Elements

We are not studying the inner life in general, with all its possible varieties, Christian or not, but only Christian spiritual life. Our necessary starting point is the dialectic of creation and incarnation, sin and redemption, which is valid in itself and independent of the hypotheses or the findings of the science of psychology. These four items (creation-incarnation, sin-redemption) may be reduced to three: nature, sin, redemption. The problem of spiritual life is to surmount the dualism between good and evil, or nature and sin; and this is done by the experience of redemption in which a dynamic principle is actively opposed to evil or sin, in that the process of divine filiation raises human nature to the realm of the life of God.

This chapter considers how the main elements of this complex are concretely to be found in Christian life.

I

NATURAL CAPACITIES OF MAN

By nature we are oriented toward God. Some elements of this relationship may be pointed out here.

1. *The Spirit.* For anyone who has understood and recognized the existence of God, being human implies the possibility of knowing and loving God. How far does this possibility go? For Thomas Aquinas (*Contra Gentes*, III), the possibility of reaching universal principles and "being as such" marks the spirit as spirit. This entails an ultimate dissatisfaction with any and all concrete beings and concrete embodiments of universal principles; nothing and nobody can fully satisfy man. This, in turn, points to an indefinite capacity of the mind which can be filled by no less than the *Infinite* (God) *finitely* apprehended.

Philosophical reflection cannot prove that such a capacity will be filled in fact. For one cannot find in man any more than a profound desire for it; human nature contains no guarantee that its thirst will be quenched. One may debate whether that capacity belongs to man's minimal ontological constitution or has somehow been superadded to it as part of his human development, but this makes little practical difference.

2. *Convergence.* Life is polarized. Each action has a direction; thus an ultimate convergence of purposes is implied in the fact that there is life. Our own life sets itself aims. All life tends toward some goal, at the very least to self-reproduction. Taken as a whole, the universe does not evolve blindly, but with a purpose. But purpose implies intention, that is, ultimately, love. Man should therefore develop his teleological sense.

3. *Ontological Dependence on God.* Both the nature of the spirit and the experience of purposeful life testify to the existence of an ontological rela-

tionship of all things with God. This can be viewed from several angles.

Fundamentally, this relationship lies in the passive aspect of creation. Creation as an act of God implies a unitive adherence of distinct beings, God and his creatures. Man's essential relationship with God involves his deepest being. It implies total dependence on man's part. Yet God remains sovereignly free and independent.

This relationship with God implies an ontological desire to know and love him. By ontological I mean that it is essential to man's very being, even when he happens to be unaware of it. The Augustinian tradition (deriving from St. Augustine through the Middle Ages) speculated that such a natural desire entails a special tie between the mind and God by way of an unconscious illumination received from him. This, however, may be questioned. One may also discuss the exact nature of that desire: Is it conditional or absolute? Does it desire God as one Creator or God as Three Persons? Is it constitutive of man's nature or an accidental perfection of it?

This natural desire of man for God is connected with his creation as image of God. All creatures are intimately related to all others insofar as they all reflect the power and goodness of God. The more profound this reflection, the more faithfully it will image its archetype. We therefore experience the desire to see God and to reflect him more adequately.

This desire is particularly connected with the Second Person, the Eternal Image, who is in God the pattern or model of creation. Thus nature itself places men in a filial position before God, like the eternal Son himself.

It is finally a presence of God in man, a presence by creative power, by immensity, and as the potential object of thought and love. Even in sin, even before the historical redemption, our desire corresponds to something in God's bending over us. God is not aloof; he attracts us.

This implies, as its counter-side, a presence of man in God. As truly as he is in us, we are in him, in his thought which creates us and guides us, in his love which wants us as his friends, in his Word through whom we were thought and created, and in his Holy Spirit, in whom we are called to holiness. We are in his life.

John Ruysbroeck expressed this by saying that from all eternity we were in his life, even though our personal existence began in time. Now we have in God an "eternal being" corresponding to our created being and to which we always aspire to be united. Our eternal being is already in God, or, perhaps better, is still in God, and our created being is in pilgrimage toward him.

4. *Awareness of God.* That there is a natural awareness of God, all Christian theologies are agreed. But not all are agreed on the extent of such an awareness. For the bishops of the First Vatican Council, the mind is able to reach knowledge of God by way of reflection on this world. With classical Thomism, every act of self-awareness contains in itself a radical knowledge of God, in the sense that its object—the self—displays a limitation in being which presupposes an infinite God distinct from, and limiting, us. For the Augustinian tradition, the knowledge of God is present in all acts of self-knowledge, for the self we know is the image of God.

However, obstacles may impede that intuitive knowledge from reaching the stages of reflection and discourse.

5. *Natural Religion.* The natural capacity to know God has given rise to many different forms of natural religions. This expression designates the sum total of beliefs and practices by which men honor God without the knowledge of his revelation in Christ. One may suspect that there is a universal pattern of natural religion, whose primal purity has been more or less defiled in local traditions. Yet it remains doubtful that strict monotheism forms the backdrop of all primitive religions. The oldest known religions are, in some way, polytheistic or pantheistic.

I would characterize natural religion by the belief in powers higher than man with whom communication is possible—especially through "ritual"—and to whom, given certain conditions, man goes after death. Belief in this invisible world creates the sense of the sacred.

Natural religion may be perverted into magic. The underlying assumption here is also the existence of a power beyond man, but with the attempt to gain mastery over it, to bend it to man's will. Thus the rituals become means of pressuring the "spirits." The sense of the sacred becomes a fear of the occult, for occult powers cannot constantly be kept at one's beck and call. Hence also the development of a caste of priests or priestesses who know the rites of initiation into the rituals and the mysteries.

One should willingly recognize that several non-Christian religions have reached a high degree of spiritualization. Without attempting to be exhaustive, I should mention here:

● *Hinduism:* focuses on the experience of inner being; it tries to give access to the hidden resources of life by way of the identity of Brahman, the great self underneath all reality, and Atman, the self of the soul.

● *Buddhism:* centers on self-identification with the inner suffering of all things; it seeks an escape from suffering by escaping from desire.

● *Islam:* centers on the uniqueness of the One God, Allah. The *Koran* teaches a religion of surrender to the supreme will of God, and the Sufi movement goes further in the direction of love for God experienced in mystical purifications.

● *Judaism:* includes strong mystical strains in the Old Testament, which are prolonged after the dispersion from Palestine. It has inspired several schools of Jewish mysticism. The Talmud speaks of many mystics among the rabbis. We should also know the Cabbalah, from the 12th to 16th centuries, and, in the 18th century, Hassidism.

I intend to describe Christian mysticism as the contemplation of the mysteries of Christ and the Trinity in the course of the development of the Christian's inner life. One may wonder at the outset if the systems of spirituality that are not founded on the revelation of Christ, but on the framework of the various world religions, can be assessed theologically in reference to the Christian mystery.

The relation of these spiritualities to ours may be seen as that of nature (or culture within the limits of the naturally given) to the revelation. Natural spirituality, and, at its summit, natural mysticism, develop natural potentialities which find their total fruition only in divine grace, but may already anticipate some of these fulfillments.

Thus, natural mysticism need not be false, although it remains incomplete. Some of the mystical writings of Hinduism and Buddhism seem to have recorded the highest point of spiritual development that can be reached outside of the revelation of Christ. The immanence of God in man may be the starting point of an acute awareness of God and the center of a very high degree of natural-cultural contemplation.

It is also possible for God to manifest himself to non-Christian mystics through special graces and to raise them to a mystical experience which is not only true, but also directly, if implicitly, related to the unique mediation of Christ. The case of the Moslem mystic Al-Hallaj seems to be an example of authentic mysticism outside of explicit Christianity.

For these reasons it may be useful, but it remains ambiguous for a Christian who aspires to union with the Three Persons to try to reach a natural contemplation of God with the help of methods that originate in non-Christian philosophies and religions, like Yoga, Zen, and their popularized versions. The danger is that, instead of true union with Christ, one may reach no more than a psychological experience of self-awareness or self-void.

The spiritual life builds upon the natural capacities of man. Hence, it should never become unnatural, but rather should correspond to man's natural capacities. The scholastic principle that "grace does not abolish, but perfects, nature" is deeply anchored in the fundamental Christian outlook on life.

A spiritual doctrine that would deny nature

would lead persons astray. One that would be satisfied with nature would not lead effectively to God, for it would stop before the end. The causes or occasions of such a failure should be investigated.

II

THE CREATOR-CREATURE CHASM

A number of hurdles stand in man's journey to God. The most elementary source of difficulties is simply the fact that we are created. Even the most perfect creatures are by definition utterly impotent of themselves to reach God. God has to give himself or he cannot be attained.

A great part of man's difficulties arise from his composite nature. Two dimensions, material and spiritual, share his psychic make-up. The resulting tension weighs upon his interior life. In its extreme forms, this tension may completely block out rational life; below that, all degrees of neuroses and psychoses have to be reckoned with, and no clear borderline distinguishes perfect psychical health from unbalance. Even in the theoretically best possible mental health, there remains the natural attraction of animality, since man is also, in his flesh, animal. A constant struggle is necessary. We cannot escape a state of tension, even if we have developed a powerful rational life, in which the mind has mastered the body.

The material and the spiritual dimensions meet in our receptive and creative imagination; through this, the realities outside of us acquire a spiritual likeness within us, in the domain proper to spirit. All things can thus wander into the inner recesses of the soul, there to be more and less spiritualized or to drag the spirit or to run around harmlessly. From this we see the need for discernment and awareness of our fantasies, the wisdom to make good use of our imaginative contents and creations, and, if necessary, the will power to check and to guide our daydreams.

The equilibrium of the component parts of personality has been further unbalanced by original sin as known in the Christian revelation. I am not concerned here with the nature, but with the effects of this sin. These may be assessed in two basically diverging ways.

First orientation: Sin has intrinsically wounded human nature, giving more pull to man's animal attractions. Due to this, many authors in the early Protestant tradition judged human nature "corrupt."

Second orientation: Man's internal disequilibrium is not worse than it would have been without original sin. The difference is that man is not merely left in his natural state; he is also deprived of God's additional gift of an easily maintained equilibrium.

In both cases, however, the human being experiences internal difficulties. Through his sense organs, he feels the attraction of what is material and physical to such a point that, in a case of conflict, he may well opt for the physical over against the spiritual. This ambiguity is the demonic wedge in him. The classical tradition in moral theology identified concupiscence (*libido*) and greed as opposed to temperance, and weakness as opposed to strength.

Man's will, attracted by sense perception, may renounce what is right (choosing maliciousness over justice).

Man's thought, influenced by sense-perception and dominated by his bent will, may prefer ignorance to knowledge (classically, ignorance to prudence).

As a result of his own sinning, each man reinforces the tensions in himself that derive from his created state, from his natural constitution and from original sin. He thus transforms bent tendencies into evil habits, which may eventually have such a hold upon him that it is all but impossible to shake them off. Insofar as they are habits, they are not necessarily willed and thus may remain free from subjective guilt; even then, however, they hinder the spiritual life and slow down its progress, for the equilibrium which they maintain is weighted toward the demonic side of man, thus stifling his spiritual dimension.

Are there any remedies to overcome the hurdles standing in the way as man journeys to God?

The remedy to man's difficulties in his spiritual development is the Christian *mystery*. All of it could be stated here, since all is relevant to our topic, but we can only sketch it in keeping with our immediate concern. We are in search of a remedy which, though it must be transcendent, should also correspond to our natural capacities.

Man being in need of a remedy to heal the gap between the two dimensions of spirit and matter in himself, and between himself and God, the remedy, called by St. Paul the "mystery," is a special presence and action of God reaching the spirit of man through matter. The reconciliation with God which follows brings about a reconciliation of spirit with matter in man and in nature. Spiritual life becomes essentially sacramental, that is, corporeal.

III
THE SACRAMENTAL LIFE

The mystery of redemption starts with the Incarnation by which the Second Person of the Trinity appears visibly in history. I must insist on the sacramental nature of the Incarnation. A sacrament may be described as a sign which contains or conveys its model or archetype. It is a comprehensive reality in which an image is in live union with its Exemplar, the image or sign belonging to the creaturely world, which is corporeal or physical, and the Exemplar being the Second Person. Such is precisely the Incarnation, where the sign is so close to God that it is God himself present in creation through a new way of being. Jesus is God-made-man: one divine Person living in one human consciousness and body, the meeting point of the Trinitarian life and of the complex of spatial and temporal, material and spiritual cross-currents which is human nature. In Jesus the abyss between God and creation is bridged; spiritual and physical creatures are at peace. Jesus not only escaped original and personal sin, but realized the spiritual capacities of human nature at its maximum. Owing to this, the tension in him between spirit and matter was no impediment to his inner life. The sacramental nature of the Incarnation was further enhanced by the sacrificial death

of Jesus, which we call Redemption. Jesus willed
his death as the central sign of his mission in men's
eyes because "there is no greater love than to give
one's life for one's friends" and also in the sight
of God; for in this human action and passion he
embodied his eternal return to the Father (*peri-
choresis*). For Christ, to die meant to go to the Father by way of the self-denial of his human nature,
on the pattern of the eternal movement by which the
Spirit and the Son are united in the Father. The
peculiar manner of his death thus becomes the rally-
ing point of mankind with God: the horizontal
branch of the Cross joins all mankind together, while
the vertical one joins creation and Creator, the four-
fold meeting point at the center being Jesus the
Christ.

From the point of view of the Incarnation and
the Redemption, it appears that only man's participation in Jesus' life, death and resurrection can fill
the gap in man's interior being; through it man can
resurrect a new man. How this is achieved we now
have to see.

In the Mystical Body of Christ, which is the
Church, the incarnational sacramental character of
salvation survives Jesus' ascension from the earth. In
it, the life of Jesus is extended to all who believe in
him. Thus, like himself, it exhibits the characteristics
of a sacrament; the Church is a special sign, in matter itself, of the presence of God in mankind. The
visibility of this sign is realized personally in the
flesh of each member of the Mystical Body, and col-
lectively in the visible union of all the faithful in
love, faith and worship. The presence of God, of
which the Ecclesial Body is the effective sign, is that

of the Second Person in Christ, of whose humanity the Mystical Body is now the sacrament. The Body of Jesus, glorified by his resurrection, is now present to all members of the Church. Owing to this sacramental nature of the Church, the Incarnation and Redemption—the life, the Cross and the Resurrection of Jesus—are as present to all the faithful at any time and in any place as they were to the disciples during Jesus' visible life on earth.

It follows that only in and through the Church can Christ be reached and the abyss between God and man be bridged.

The sacramental structure of the ecclesial way of salvation has to be made practically recognizable and the Divine Reality attainable. To this end they are mediated by a number of sacraments. Each sacrament achieves the incarnate presence of God in mankind through Christ and his Mystical Body for the benefit of each Christian in the concrete circumstances of his life. Some are of general use, aiming at renewing and making the presence of God closer (Baptism, Confirmation, Eucharist), while others make us perceive his presence at some particular occasion or function. It also follows that the sacraments refer us to the life of Christ, whence the legitimacy of the symbolism by which each evokes a certain attitude of Jesus in his life, which is the real content of the idea of their institution by Jesus: they correspond to his explicit or implicit intentions. For example:

Baptism—Death and Resurrection
Confirmation—Sending of the Holy Spirit
Eucharist—Self-sacrifice in the communion meal

Holy Orders—Self-sacrifice as a function of mediation

Penance and the Sacrament of the Sick—Forgiveness of sins and healing

Marriage—Transfiguration of the flesh

The Sacraments of Initiation:
Baptism, Confirmation, Eucharist

The believer participates in the life of Christ chiefly through the three sacraments of initiation. In Baptism, he participates in the death and resurrection of Christ, thus dying in principle to the world (that is, to that in himself which is demonic and keeps him from total unity with God) and resurrecting to new life with God (that is, to a new purpose in his life, a new action and witness in his behavior, a new knowledge and concern in his intellect, a new hope in his memory and a new center in his imagination). In Confirmation, he receives the Spirit, thus pursuing his participation in the Trinitarian life. In the Eucharist, the believer shares with Christ the fruit of his sacrifice, participating in the resurrected and glorious life of the divine humanity of the one who became, at his ascension, the Lord of heaven and earth.

Whether received once, like Baptism and Confirmation, or frequently, as the Eucharist ought to be received, the sacraments of initiation are permanent realities at the heart of the inner life. We should not only receive them or simply have the abstract knowledge that we have received them, as is often the case with Baptism. We should frequently think of this

abiding presence in us and of our continuing participation in the death and resurrection of Christ, in the
gift of the Spirit, in the glory of the resurrected Lord
manifested in the eucharistic *koinonia*.

Penance

Penance and the Sacrament of the Sick belong
together as sacraments of healing. The advent of scientific medicine has effectively killed the latter as a
means of bodily healing normally active in the spiritual life of the faithful. With the advent of scientific
psychology and psychiatry, penance runs the danger
of also dying as a means of psychological healing to
which we have recourse when we experience guilt.
For this reason, a new type of ritual for this sacrament is of immediate urgency. For its demise would
deprive the Christian of a means of access to Christ
the healer, who gave his life for the sins of the world
and also for the quieting of the guilty conscience
which is the consequence of sin and the result of the
experience of sinning. Penance is an encounter with
Christ for reconciliation with God, with the community and with oneself. The gesture of forgiveness as-
sures us of the continuing fidelity of God and of the
permanence of the fruits of Redemption. The believer seeks it with the same faith he seeks Christ.
For the Savior must be known as doctor and healer
of the distressed soul, compassionate for our
weakness, understanding our failures and falls, and
intimate with the most hidden secrets of our hearts,
no less than as the Lord of heaven and earth.

Marriage

For the majority of the faithful, the sacrament of marriage provides the framework of adult life and should therefore be one of the most powerful aids in their search for holiness. In this sacrament man and wife are united to each other as to Christ. That is, the actions of love that strengthen their oneness should be lived as those of Christ manifesting his tenderness through the tenderness of a human partner. This requires a gift of self in the daily routine of living, and demands a spiritualization of sex as opening onto the experience of the sacred. That marriage is, for the Catholic Church, a sacrament of the Gospel means that it is not only a natural relationship, but also a way of holiness. Its sufferings are those of Christ in us, or, conversely, our participation in the sufferings of Christ. Its joy, in all its spiritual, emotional and physical aspects, anticipates the eschatological fulfillment and the entrance of the faithful into the heavenly joy of God himself. One can hardly exaggerate the spiritual possibilities of sacramental marriage if the two partners are equally eager to develop its interior dimension toward peace, harmony, mutual obedience and joy in the Spirit.

There follows a commitment to the world and to creation, the experience of marriage and community life in the family throwing light upon the proper socialization of society and the communion of saints in the Church.

By the sacramental life, God is ever present to us through Christ in the Church, his Mystical Body.

IV
THE LITURGICAL LIFE

This is not a new topic. The liturgical life is an extension of the sacramental life. Because the organ of salvation is sacramental and incarnational, the Church is liturgical and doxological. The relations between liturgy and Church are so close that it is absolutely impossible to lead a normal Christian life without a minimal liturgical experience. The deeper the latter, the more vigorous the former. This could be shown by a study of a few typical saints; yet I am not primarily concerned with factual reports about what others, even saints, have done, but with a normative investigation of what should be done according to the nature of things. I will, therefore, proceed to an intrinsic study of the nature of the liturgy.

The Liturgy from the Viewpoint of Its Origin

In the divine plan of salvation, the Christian liturgy was destined to supersede the imperfect liturgical life of the temple. At the same time, some of the culture of the temple was bound to remain; in spite of the unavoidable discontinuity between the Old Testament and the New, the latter evolved from the former, in which it was cradled until it was sociologically strong enough to break with the old Israel, a break which was symbolized by the destruction of Jerusalem in 70. Not only the temple but the other Jewish religious institutions as well, particularly the synagogue and the congregations of "anawim," influenced Christian origins. All this should be kept in mind for an appreciation of the liturgy. For our present purpose it will suffice to suggest the main aspects of temple worship and to mention other Jewish influences which seem to have been felt in the formation of an independent Christian liturgy.

Worship at the temple had two chief aspects. On the one hand, it was the worship of Yahweh. From this point of view, its center was the sacrifice regulated by laws or customs deemed to be God-given. Those rites, however, drew their holiness, not from themselves, but from the fact that they were tokens of the continuity of the covenant with Abraham. Abraham killed a bull, cut it in two and walked in between, and Yahweh passed through it after him. Moses offered sacrifice in the wilderness during that golden age of friendship with Yahweh. Elias' victims were consumed by a fire from heaven. Thus the covenant was preserved century after century. With the construction of the temple, the covenant centered in the Holy of Holies, at the spot where Yahweh is present, receives prayers and sacrifices and constantly renews the covenant. Thus, we should note particularly the notion of the presence of Yahweh in faithfulness to the covenant.

On the other hand, the temple itself became the object of a cult, as the result of a spontaneous veneration (Ezekiel and his enthusiastic description of the temple). The temple became a symbol and instrument of the covenant; the Jews in exile dreamt of it; the Jews of the Diaspora went on pilgrimage to it. It remained the sign of the unity of the Jewish people around God, in spite of their political subjection.

The apocalyptic literature developed the theme of the woman-temple, which was embodied in the Apocalypse of John. Thus, the cult in the temple of Jerusalem was related to the eternal adoration of God to be realized eschatologically. There was a tendency to equate earth and heaven, the temple and the heavenly Jerusalem, as far as worship was concerned. This will provide one of the basic principles of the Christian liturgy.

Besides the temple, there was in post-exilic Judaism the synagogue which became an essential element in Jewish life. It is relevant to our study insofar as it promoted a cult of the Bible, of the Word. A synagogue meeting was mainly devoted to reading and commenting on the Bible. Thus, the Bible became more than a ritual for the worship of Yahweh, which it is in its ceremonial sections; it acquired mediatory value, interposed between Yahweh and the people, and conveying the words of Yahweh. Here we touch upon the origin of the concept of inspired writings, which translates the experience of the synagogue and, before that, of the Exile when a power from God was perceived in the words of Torah and the older prophets. Thus, the texts of the Old Testament, which could already be read as history, poetry, or prophecy, became essentially prophetic in their interpretation by the synagogue. They were received as messages from God, a process which was later extended to the New Testament. The Bible was the work of listeners and readers as well as of writers. All the people who were inspired in and through its use contributed to its inspiration.

Finally, the *anawim* developed a community worship on a small scale characterized by a spiritualization of the notion of sacrifice. This became the sacrifice of the heart and was expressed in common actions by the members of the brotherhood—chanting psalms, eating religious meals, etc. Thus a semi-official institution was set up, in which ritual regulated meetings and sacred meals. Important traces of this linger on in the Gospels, Jesus being the leader of one such brotherhood and the Last Supper one of those sacred meals. However important this may have been in Jewish life and in the life of Jesus, it is now a side issue for us. It is worth noting, however, that in these confraternities the religious life of the people was handed on in its purity. Hope in a small remnant inspired many of them, and their meditation was focused precisely on those passages of the Bible which were germane to *anav* piety, especially the psalms and the second Isaiah.

Purification and Perfection by Jesus Christ

Those various elements were sifted by Jesus, who selected a few to be maintained and drew inspiration from them to bring about a radical transformation of the cult. The principle of that purification is to be found in the promise that "the time is coming when the true adorers will adore in spirit and truth" (John). Jesus holds the Jews to adore "in truth" while his own function is to ensure adoration not only "in truth" but "in spirit" also.

Jesus maintained and transformed the following:

1. the idea of a ritual cult, including sacrifices.

The cult in the temple was detached from its traditional setting and from the Mosaic ritual and focused on the presence of God in the small remnant.

2. the idea of a worship of the temple, the temple being Jesus himself. This point will be stressed by Paul and in the Apocalypse of John.

3. the idea that God speaks to the people through the words of the Bible. This is implied in the use of the Old Testament. It is taken up by the disciples in their organization of the synaxis or liturgical meeting. There is, however, a new interpretation of the Bible, now read in the light of the words of Jesus.

4. the idea of a sacred meal as the main element of the Christian ritual as of the *anav* meeting.

All that was transformed. In the cult of the early Church the liturgy was made of two main elements.

First, at the beginning of the meeting, though this may have been, at some time and in some places, a separate meeting, there is worship of the Lord speaking through the Bible, to which the New Testament came, little by little, to be equated. The Word is present in the Bible, that is, not in the material book, or in the letter as distinct from the meaning, but in the spiritual understanding that the Church has of it. The encounter of the believing mind and the inspired text is the starting point of a further inspiration: the Word of God becomes present to the people.

Second, after Bible worship, there takes place a complex action in which the notions of the presence of Yahweh, of sacrifice, of temple worship, and of sacred meal converge upon an awareness of the

Word as God himself, as sacrifice, as heavenly temple, and as sacred food. The link between those apparently differing ideas may derive from a meditation on the manna given by Yahweh to the Hebrews. Jesus is the true manna, coming from heaven, given to the true Israel. Thus, he has made himself food and drink, the two elements that supply all needs, like manna. Christians therefore will have a sacred meal, independent of the old temple, because the true temple is Jesus Christ himself, in whom God is present, "reconciling the world to himself" by the spiritual sacrifice.

Character of the New Cult

From what precedes, this may be reduced to two heads: it is true and spiritual—true insofar as it perfectly achieves what it means; spiritual in that, its focal point being Jesus Christ in his resurrected body, it takes place on two planes: the earthly in which the Christian community lives and the action takes place, and the heavenly, in which Christ is and the reality signified by the action is performed. Thus, the Christian liturgy implies a participation in the heavenly, an ascent of the earthly Jerusalem to the heavenly, an anticipation of the eschatological destiny of man, when the eternal image of the Church will simply coincide with its temporal counterpart. This eschatological aspect was central to the piety of the first Christians.

From the point of view of the cult of the Word, it is also true and spiritual—true because it is a cult of the true message by which God has been present to the new Israel, spiritual because it now guarantees the spiritual meaning of the Bible, the Spirit of God, Jesus Christ understood in the light of the Holy Spirit.

From both viewpoints, the new cult appears as essentially corporate. It is the liturgy of a collectivity, the new Israel. Certainly, individual Christians are destined to reach sanctity through it. Yet the aim is not their sanctification; it is the worship of God through the only Mediator in the only Church. This shows, incidentally, that sanctification is not a self-centered activity, even though it should properly develop self-knowledge and introspection. It is God-centered, with no coming back upon self, at least in prayer itself.

The Liturgy from the Viewpoint of Its Development

The striking element in the development of the liturgical forms of worship is the growth of the liturgical year. At the beginning, the Christians only commemorated the death and resurrection of the Lord; all Eucharists were commemorations of this, as they still are. Little by little, other elements were differentiated. Since the Eucharist was celebrated on Sunday, Sunday remained particularly devoted to the resurrection. During the first three centuries, other elements emerged. The biblical texts to be read originally followed a Jewish pattern and were chosen independently for their suitability to the mystery.

There were commemorations of special mysteries of the life of Jesus; there were others devoted to the praise of the *Theotokos* and the memory of the martyrs. Little by little, the primitive pattern gave place to an elaborate one, a process which was hastened by apologetic necessity; the Christianization of pagan feasts was an important factor in the rise of some major feasts, like Christmas. Each period has tended to add new elements to emphasize some spiritual insights or to celebrate new saints.

Thus, the liturgy results from a deepening grasp of the wealth of the central mystery: all worship remains illuminated by the death and resurrection of Jesus, which is looked at in manifold ways because of its manifold aspects. It illustrates the life of the Mystical Body, which spontaneously patterns itself on the mystery of the divine Person in the human life of Christ.

This is closely tied to the sacramental life, the meaning of which is made manifest in worship. The sacraments give life to the wider framework which embraces all life and all creation. The Eucharist is also the center of worship. As Christ remains present to the Church through the sacraments, so in the liturgy the Church lives symbolically, typically, the very life of Jesus. Commemorating the events of his life on earth and in his saints and his heavenly glory, the Church participates in them. The perfect worship of the Father, having been achieved in Jesus, is now effectively symbolized in the liturgy. By this participation in Christ, the Mystical Body achieves also its perfect adoration, which is identically that of the Son, first-born of many brethren.

V

MAIN ELEMENTS OF THE LITURGY

The Central Action: The Mass

Let us now consider the main elements of the liturgy, such as they should be understood to help our interior life. They should not be extrinsic supports; rather, in and by them the spiritual life will be nurtured, even unawares. The main element, by which the liturgy is directly part of the sacramental order, is the Eucharistic celebration.

Let us look at the two parts of the Eucharist.

A cult of the Word, the remnant perhaps of an independent service, forms the subject matter of a biblical cycle of readings. The reading of the Bible is an essential part of the relationship between the Church and Christ; the Church keeps the Scriptures that speak of him, and feeds on them in the corporate action at the beginning of Mass. It is in relation to that corporate reading that the Bible finds its spiritual meaning which emerges from the encounter of the Church reading and of Christ read. That Christ is not present in the text as such is no hindrance to a real communion of love. The soul communicates with the Spirit of Christ while the mind reads through the body. By Spirit of Christ I mean not only the doctrine and intentions of Jesus, but also his Holy Spirit, who gives the understanding of Jesus' doctrines and actions.

Thus we have occasion to be united with Christ in the spiritual sense of the texts speaking of him. This not only prepares the Eucharistic communion;

it also has an intrinsic value: it achieves a spiritual union between Christ and ourselves as his spiritual body; it realizes the mystery of the presence of Christ in his Church. And, as already said, the whole plan of salvation revolves round the idea of achieving a new Presence of God among men.

The Eucharistic part of the Mass has in fact become the focal point of many schools of spirituality, often called eucharistic. The design of God is to bridge the gap between God and man by the Incarnation and the correlative elevation and deification of man. The sacraments make Christ's presence in mankind effective for those who are thereby united to some aspects of the mystery of Christ. The relation between God, Christ and mankind was ultimately expressed on the Cross at the self-sacrifice of Jesus for men. The Mass relates us to this event by renewing the offering of bread and wine by which, at the Last Supper, our Lord anticipated his death on the Cross ("This is my blood . . . given for you") and his resurrection as spiritual food. Jesus is now the Lamb under the appearance of bread and wine. He is the temple. He is the priest. Thus the Mass is a sacrifice, insofar as Jesus is present in it in his crucified, though now glorious, flesh. There is no further immolation, but Christ is present as spiritual food under the symbols of human food. Communion to the body and blood of Jesus is our participation in the mystical (because realized in a "mystery") union between Christ and the Church, a participation which is made through eating, the soul receiving the Lord as the body receives the food.

Clearly one cannot separate sacrifice and sacrament: the Eucharist is the sacrament of a sacrifice. It may be said to renew the sacrifice of Calvary, because it effectively makes it present. Yet it is not a new sacrifice. The only Christian sacrifice took place historically on Golgotha and takes place sacramentally on the altar, that is, in the body of Christ, the only real altar of the new cult, when the Church's prayer over bread and wine recalls his self-offering to the Father.

One may wonder what are the best conditions for a fruitful communion. The only real participation in the Eucharist is communion. Following or saying the prayers is good, and may be subjectively fruitful. But communion alone is the sacramental means of sharing. Admittedly, communion should be prepared for by prayer, but prayer itself receives its full meaning from communion.

Communion, entailing the presence of Jesus Christ in and with us, ensures the forgiveness of sins, often signified by an absolution at the beginning, but achieved in communion itself. There is little sense in abstaining from communion because of spiritual estrangement and guilt, since this is precisely the food of healing. For this reason, many mystics have presented the Eucharist as the sacrament for the unitive way. This does not mean that it is reserved to those who already are in the unitive way, but that it more particularly helps to become and remain united to God. There are close relations between Eucharistic communion and mystical union to God.

The Liturgical Cycle

This is the general sequence of readings and prayers in the first part of Mass, Scripture being read in keeping with the mood of each liturgical season, and the prayers being planned as a mystical participation in the main events of salvation history: Advent (Old Testament), Christmastide, the life of Christ upon earth till Easter, Pentecost (the gift of the Spirit), and the history of the Church after Pentecost, seen as a deepening of the Scriptures and an expectation of the End.

I am concerned here with the spiritual, not the historical aspect of this: it offers a remarkable occasion of deepening our understanding of the Word of God present through the reading of the Bible. In Advent, Christ is present among those who expect his coming in the mystery of the divine preparation of mankind for the Incarnation. The whole liturgical cycle achieves the presence of Christ in his Church according to the many aspects of his mystery.

Protestant piety has excessively lost the sense of the Eucharistic presence, yet genuinely retained the sense of the scriptural presence of the Lord, when the Scriptures are read as a means of communion with Christ. The popular tendency of Catholic piety has been to leave the scriptural presence aside and focus attention on the sacrament. Yet this tendency runs counter to the insistence of the great Catholic mystics on the spiritual meaning of the Bible and on the relation between the scriptural and the sacramental presences. These are not subordinated one to another; but they jointly unveil two aspects of the mystery of Christ, namely his sacrifice and the transformation of all things by the Incarnation.

The Office

While the Eucharistic service is, in its first part,

a *reading* of and listening to Scripture and, in its second part, a *participation* in the Sacrifice of Christ, the office is a *prayer* by which the Church unites itself to the prayer of Christ. Hence its main characteristics as a prayer of praise, rather than of petition, for Christ has nothing to ask for: he has only to praise the Father, to look at him; and as biblical prayer based upon the psalms, since these themselves are the scriptural expression of the eternal prayer of the Word, as they were Jesus' prayers on earth. Thus, the Church unites itself to the Word in the movement by which, having assumed all things, he presents them to the Father. This he symbolized and expressed in the Psalms, where all human emotions (love of God, of men, of friends, of family, admiration, unhappiness, illness, even hatred) are assumed and presented to God in praise.

The form taken by this prayer results from historical contingencies. It is, however, focused upon the Eucharistic sacrifice offered halfway between the two halves of history, between the Old and the New Covenant. Communion with the scriptural and the Eucharistic mysteries is at the center of our communion with the prayer of the Word of God. This is one more instance of the union between Christ and his mystical body which is the essence of the Christian mystery.

VI

THE IMPORTANCE OF HOLY SCRIPTURE

The liturgical life has introduced us already to the Bible as one of the expressions of the presence of God with us and one of the means by which this presence becomes a dialogue. The relevance of the Scriptures is not exhausted by its place in liturgical worship. There is still room for reading the written Word of God on our own initiative, with the purpose of learning to understand God's design upon us better, of finding strength and consolation in the trials and tests we may be subjected to, and of learning to respond to God's demands and calls.

The basis for this biblical dimension of the Christian life is apparent in the reflection that, unlike man, who needs to improve himself through experience, God's purpose is total from the beginning. Even though it has been revealed to man gradually through the history of salvation, it takes the form, in human history and consciousness, of a developing model rather than that of successive models following each other as the latest displaces the one before. Finally, the fullness of God's design was manifested for all future times in the coming of Jesus Christ, the Word made flesh. God has now spoken his entire Word. Nothing more can be added to the revelation of the Incarnate Lord, who is, in his very person and function, God's ultimate and final intention.

No event in the later history of the Church can replace, add to, or subtract from what is already given to us in Jesus Christ. And therefore no writing, statement, creed, or definition of faith can add anything to what is spoken to us in the Scriptures.

Several passages of the Bible have exercised a special attraction for Christians in the development of their interior journey. In the Old Testament, the Psalms, the Song of Songs, the books of the prophets, and the Book of Wisdom have always inspired the Christian mystics. To some extent, they them-

selves describe the mystical dimension of the Old
Testament, when God speaks to his people and inspires its response of love, obedience and fidelity. In
the New Testament, the Epistles of St. Paul record
his own spiritual experience and explain the mystical
dimension of the life lived in and with Christ. The
Johannine writings, besides providing many profound insights into the mystery of Christ, contain the
mystical promise: "Anyone who loves me will be
true to my word, and my Father will love him; we
will come to him and make our dwelling place with
him" (Jn. 14:23). In the synoptic Gospels, the Beatitudes have been taken as the charter of the life leading to intimacy with God, and the account of the
transfiguration as the symbolic expression of the
crowning point of the interior life.

It is up to each of the faithful to discover the
biblical passages that speak to him more tellingly of
the mercies of God, of the love of Christ and of the
transforming power of the Spirit. One should read
the Bible frequently, not with the sense of fulfilling
an obligation that would be otherwise unpleasant,
but with the perseverance and expectation of one
who is always content with seeking the Lord,
whether the Lord shows himself or not.

Admittedly, a technical initiation is necessary to
a scientific reading of the Scriptures. But the relevance of the Scriptures to the interior life is not com-
mensurate with the accuracy of our understanding of
it. There is an understanding at the level of the text;
this requires as much historical and philological
science as we can master. But there is another level
of understanding, in which we perceive the Word
speaking rather than the words spoken. For this,

love for God, docility to the Spirit, concern for the mind of Christ, distrust of our own imagining, eagerness to learn and readiness to be corrected are more effective instruments of knowledge than scientific investigation.

It is at this level that spiritual authors, following many theologians, have spoken of the spiritual sense of the Bible. This is not an esoteric, hidden meaning, which would be transmitted in secret or discovered by some privileged minds. It results from the interiorization in the Christian soul of the mysteries related, or alluded to, in the Scriptures. Such an interiorization always follows the lines of thought and behavior represented by faith, love and hope: faith accepts and believes Christ; love unites to God; hope seeks for him.

VII
INTERIOR PRAYER

Mental or interior prayer should not be separated from the sacramental and liturgical life. For sanctification, our participation in the fullness of salvation, does not follow two paths, the one sacramental and liturgical, the other derived from an ascetical effort directed by psychological laws. Psychology is good for prayer as long as it remains subordinate to theology, but it should not be a rival of liturgy or sacrament.

Yet the sacraments and the liturgy do not cover all aspects of mental prayer, and interior life should amount to more than a faithful practice of the sacraments and the liturgy. Or it would hurt a basic element of the interior life, namely its orientation toward the contemplation of the mystery of God, which is not exhausted by its liturgical expression.

The doctrine on interior prayer that I propose rests on the principle that the sacraments and the liturgy are the two main objective constituents of the spiritual life. Objectively speaking, they are sufficient to bridge the gap between God and man. As a result, they promote a personal grasp of the presence of God, which obeys laws of its own and follows principles still to be determined. This is a personal, subjective element, even though these laws and principles originate in the gift of the divine life to man in Baptism. Consequently, I should say a few words on the origin of interior prayer, its structure, its forms, and the differentiation of "schools" on the practice of interior prayer.

Origin of Interior Prayer

The liturgical life is an extension of the sacramental life. Interior prayer is a further extension of it. But it derives also from the natural capacities of man.

The natural capacities of man, that is, his nature as flesh and spirit, his talents, his fundamental relation to God, his awareness of God, the assumption and practices of natural religion, already place man on the way to God and make the development of the presence of God possible. It would be a misreading of this to fall back upon purely natural wisdom and psychological exercises to sharpen this orientation; one would thus miss the real issue, which is to transcend the limitations of one's own self and reach beyond what self-development can achieve. However, once Christ has taken hold of a human being through the sacramental order, his natural capacities are still present. By introspection, interior quiet and constant watch, they may be stretched to their utmost limit. The natural awareness of God can then be sharpened by knowledge of God in faith, interpreted in its light and systematically sublimated.

This is the beginning of interior prayer. Even before a child is acquainted with the sacraments (although he is already, by Baptism, in the sacramental order), his first acts of faith, however imperfect in their formulation and, perhaps, not yet formulated, make him aware of the hidden presence of God behind everything and lead him to adore God in his childlike fashion.

This first stage of interior prayer may later be choked by social pressure, or on the contrary it can develop through the experience of the sacraments.

The sacramental life—especially through the sacraments already received by children: Confirmation, Eucharist, Penance—then fosters a higher spiritual life, more elaborate and based on a deeper knowledge of God, but running the risk of self-consciousness and pride. It is not, at that time, systematic; no times are set apart for prayer. Reduced to a more or less fervent practice of the sacraments, with frequent short moments of prayer and thanksgiving, it is enough to preserve the usual awareness of the presence of God. It shows itself usually in the child as the idea, not of spending more time in prayer, but of doing things for and with God. It can be the origin of a kind of meditation, as a very simple occasional reflection on God. Eventually, among adults, interior prayer may emerge from sacramental life as a more systematic prayer and a more careful attention to the presence of God.

What liturgical life tends to add to this is to prolong interior prayer: it extends its practice to all life and not only to the special moments when we receive the sacraments, and it centers it upon the essential. When liturgical life is being developed, and in the occasional but conscious reception of the sacraments, interior prayer is tantamount to a sense of the presence of God. While it feeds upon the objective data of the natural and the sacramental order, it also obeys laws of its own, revealing a special dimension of our interior spirit.

Structure of Mental Prayer

The purpose of interior prayer is to achieve in a personal life what the sacraments and the liturgy have already achieved for the Christian community as a whole. It fosters awareness of the presence of God in us—more exactly, of the presence of the Three Persons revealed in Jesus Christ.

This presence of God has a natural basis, yet it is beyond the limits of nature. Accordingly the means through which one will be aware of it must also transcend nature, for there should be a proportion between the means and the end. In the structure of grace, this knowledge of the presence of God is ensured by the points of direct contact which we have with the Trinity: faith, love and hope. Interior prayer results from the activity of these. It consists in believing, loving and hoping, in relation to the Tri-Une God. In whatever way we do this, the purpose must never be lost sight of. Without it, the most elaborate methods would be in vain, and results a delusion.

It follows that interior prayer is not:

- a mere feat of imagination;
- a mere control of the body;
- an intellectual activity;
- a psychological introspection;
- a rational knowledge of God;
- a blind experience or a bizarre interior feeling.

It is a theological knowledge of God only insofar as theology helps to develop faith and inspires *loving* knowledge of the Three Persons. The study of theology in the right spirit is extremely valuable to reach an habitual state of interior prayer.

Forms of Interior Prayer

The diversification of forms of interior prayer may be made along two ways.

Horizontally: Several forms of interior prayer may co-exist. Since it originates in the life of Baptism, it can be simply a consciousness of our sacramental and liturgical life. We live sacramentally, and all our efforts tend to bring more fervor into this life. The sacraments and liturgy are then not only the origin, but also the constant food and the goal of interior prayer. One may term this a pre-systematic prayer (I).

In a more organized, yet still largely spontaneous state, interior prayer simply nourishes the development of faith, love and hope in all their scope, though with no specific method. This is also pre-systematic: but, instead of being focused upon the objective data of the order revealed in Christ, it is centered on the subjective, inner paths leading to them, faith, love and hope (II). In practice, (I) and (II) are always joined, though the stress may bear on the one or the other. In either case, interior prayer brings into one the threefold path within oneself and the revealed realities, especially in their sacramental aspects. (I) sees faith, love and hope as ways to share in the sacramentality of revelation; (II) sees the sacramental order as the new level of redeemed mankind, which has to be personally experienced through faith, love and hope.

Finally, interior prayer at times seems to be partly detached from its sacramental origin and from the theological virtues, and to stress the elements of the human psyche that are operative in prayer (III). This remains oriented to contemplation if the themes of its reflection are still those of the revelation. This more systematic form of prayer can be manifold, according to the diversity of its psychic supports and of the themes considered. For instance, there is room for a more intellectual and a more affective emphasis.

(I) and (II) may be termed the classical forms of pre-Reformation theology and spirituality. It is that of the Fathers, the medieval theologians, and monastic orders. (III), popularized by the followers of the *Devotio moderna* and, later, by the Counter-Reformation, has obtained priority in most modern Catholic writings on the interior life.

Vertically: Interior prayer also, and this is much more important, develops upward, through stages that may be, to some extent, mapped out, toward higher levels of perfection; or, to use another metaphor, it develops inwardly, reaching toward a more interior centrality. That aim, and the journey toward it, may be described, both with the help of theological reflection and from the records left by mystics who were able to analyze their interior itinerary. A comparison of these writings shows that progress follows a similar pattern in most cases although this is diversified in minor points. This outline is often presented under the trilogy—purgative, illuminative, unitive ways—though these are not exactly successive, and they so overlap that there is never a purely purgative, illuminative, or unitive stage of interior life.

Another classification of the inner life is focused, not on the main immediate aim to be achieved (purity, illumination, union), but on the form of prayer that is being experienced—meditation, simplified prayer, contemplation.

Finally, there may be subdivisions within each of these three stages. Although they are not of immediate relevance to most of the faithful, an acquaintance with them is useful.

Sharing Interior Prayer

The heart caught up in prayer and united to

God may well be filled to overflowing. It likes to share its fullness with others and it may wish to exteriorize its prayer. Liturgical worship provides a natural context for this, especially through singing, through the formal responses made in common, and through spontaneous intercessions during the "prayer of the faithful."

But more spontaneous exteriorization may also take place in the fullness of interior prayer. Prayer groups or prayer meetings are often focused on the experience of shared prayer. Participation in such groups may serve as a means of growth in prayer.

Shared prayer takes many forms:

• witnessing to the action of divine grace in one's life; long practiced in some Protestant Churches, this has a legitimate place in any group that feels close enough for this sharing to be made freely and comfortably;

• praying for the spiritual and material needs of oneself and others; this prayer of petition has been familiar to Catholics for a long time;

• expressing the joy of adoration, knowledge and experience of God, and giving thanks for them;

• expressing adoration, knowledge and experience of God with joy; this is related to the former but requires a greater familiarity with the experience of personal prayer in public.

The felt need to share prayer may not be sufficiently met by the infrequent opportunities provided in official liturgical contexts. Groups where personal spontaneity is more or less expected can fulfill this need. While they do not replace liturgical worship and do not compete with parish services, they provide valuable contexts for shared prayer in its most spontaneous forms. The multiplication of prayer groups is an important sign of the times: the Spirit calls us to deeper prayer.

Speaking in Tongues

This has a long history: it is mentioned in St. Paul's First Epistle to the Corinthians, chapters 12-14 (where Paul tries to regulate its practice) and in the Acts of the Apostles, chapters 2 and 10 (where it is connected with baptism and shows that baptism with water is also baptism with the Holy Spirit). Around the years 50 (at Corinth) and 80-90 (in Acts), speaking in tongues was therefore known as a frequent phenomenon in the prayer meetings of Christians. It disappeared from usual practice in subsequent centuries, although it is occasionally mentioned: in the times of the Fathers of the Church (in connection with Montanism); in the Middle Ages in the lives of several mystics (such as Angela de Foligno in thirteenth-century Italy or Margerie Kempe in fourteenth-century England). After becoming part of the normal prayer pattern of some small Protestant groups it entered the main Protestant Churches by way of the revivals of the eighteenth and nineteenth centuries in America. More recently it has become a feature of the renovation of prayer in some Lutheran and Anglican Churches and in the Catholic Church.

Speaking in tongues consists in uttering sounds that are not part of any language, yet that have, for the speaker and for some of the listeners, a symbolic meaning relating to prayer. It may derive from a deep prayer which, for many possible reasons, does not find expression in language. It may express the need for a sacred tongue which is no longer met by vernacular liturgies. It may be due to a psychological need for spontaneity and freedom that is impeded by the conventionalities of language. It may express an eschatological longing for the "new tongues" promised in Mark 16:17. Or it may even be a fashion or a fad. All of these possible explanations can also be given for the "gift of tears," which was frequent in Christian piety in the last few centuries.

It is debatable whether speaking in tongues ought to be desired by those who wish for a more fervent prayer. For the sources and causes of this experience are still too uncertain, as are also its effects. Is speaking in tongues a means of progress? A mark of already achieved progress? A phenomenon that is neither good nor bad but can be used either way, for good and for bad? A happening that is inspired by the Holy Spirit? A natural form of self-expression analogous to song, poetry or dance? In more theological terms, is it an actual grace given as a token of God's love and presence? A normal flowering of sanctifying grace in certain conditions? A grace "graciously given" (*gratia gratis data*) for a specific function? That it may be a "charism"—that is, a gift from God—does not lift all ambiguity, since the Christian life is filled with charisms of all sorts.

On the one hand, speaking in tongues, like the former gift of tears, has played a positive role in the life of many. On the other, the common doctrine of the great Christian mystics is to ignore such phe-

nomena, even if they are God-given. It therefore
seems that two principles ought to be kept:

1. the principle of St. Paul, that in the worship
assembly one should not speak in tongues unless an
interpreter can explain the meaning for the sake of
the community (1 Cor. 14:28);

2. the principle of St. John of the Cross, that
one should not be attached to spiritual gifts from
God, for the only "proper and proportionate" means
of union to God is faith (*The Ascent of Mount Carmel*, part II, chapter VIII).

Spiritual Schools on Interior Prayer

Since the interior life may be seen from different angles, there are different outlooks on its
practice and also, to some extent, on the constituents
of its higher levels. Three general principles of differentiation may be pointed out:

(a) the predominance of one of the three views
given on mental prayer and its relation to faith, love
and hope and to the sacramental order;

(b) the selection of some themes as the most
helpful or adequate;

(c) yet this is not all; for differing theological
positions may also inspire diverse stresses in spirituality.

Those three lines of cleavage being kept in
mind, one may arrive at several classifications of
spiritual schools.

According to (a): patristic spirituality (Benedic-
tine); medieval spirituality (that is, most Orders in
the strict sense of the term: e.g., Dominicans, Fran-

ciscans, Carmelites, etc.); modern spirituality (*Devotio moderna*, Jesuits).

According to (b): spiritualities centered upon a special mystery or a particular aspect of Christianity, such as the French School (seventeenth century), centered upon the hypostatic union (Bérulle) or adoration with the Supreme Adorer, Christ (Ollier); the Congregations (founded mainly in the nineteenth century).

According to (c): spiritualities based on the hypothesis of a universal call to contemplation (Thomism) or on the contrary hypothesis (many Jesuit authors) or on a middle position (as in the Carmel tradition). Other points of divergence are: the possibility or not of acquired contemplation; the primacy of intellect or of love; the nature of the gifts of the Holy Spirit.

Conclusion

It follows from the preceding pages that I do not equate interior prayer with a specific exercise of piety to be connumerated with other sacramental and liturgical exercises; rather I see it as the outcome of all serious sacramental and liturgical life. It is man's share in God's design to bridge the gap between himself and creation. This design being essentially incarnational—and, as a result, sacramental and liturgical—the inner life consists in being admitted to an experience of the renovation of all things initiated by the Incarnation. This is achieved through the sacraments, which are the principles of a wider sacramental outlook upon all things, to be developed through a deeply felt participation in worship. Interior prayer is the psychological aspect of the inner life, that is, that part of it which falls within the scope of introspection and self-analysis.

In this perspective, interior prayer cannot be identified, as is often done, with meditation. Such a restriction could be accepted if interior prayer was a specific exercise; and, admittedly, such a concept has influenced many treatises on prayer. I do not intend to underrate the practice of mental prayer at any time; yet I would maintain that even when it is practiced outside of a liturgical or sacramental context, it is not an exercise by itself. Interior prayer is the experiential aspect of all spiritual life, and spiritual life is man's participation in the incarnational design of salvation and sanctification.

3
Dynamic Principles

The remedy to man's defectiveness and irresponsibility, which doom his attempt at union with God, does not lie only in God's entrance into the human order. This is an objective prerequisite of salvation; but it would not solve the problem if, at the same time, man were not correspondingly fitted with a special strengthening of his natural capacity. This is the subjective means of elevation toward the divine order. It also provides the principle of the development of the inner life.

This strengthening is effected by what I call the dynamic principles of the interior life, whose classical sequence is: *grace, theological virtues, moral virtues, gifts of the Holy Spirit.* In order to stress what is primary, I will speak of the theological virtues—faith, love and hope—adding short studies on the gifts of the Holy Spirit and on some of the moral virtues.

Baptism introduces the Christian into the order of redemption and sanctification. It also equips him with the subjective means of life with God. God is present in him; this is the objective presence of God, or the immediate result of it in the soul, which is now made "like" God. Classical theology explained this likeness as an infused quality affecting the substance of the soul, which it called sanctifying grace.

Grace now enables man to live with God and for him. His inner faculties of action are transformed by what classical theology called the *theological virtues:* faith, corresponding to intellect; hope, corresponding to memory; love, corresponding to will. Thanks to these, a direct contact can be established with God present in the soul. The structure of that contact needs to be analyzed.

I
FAITH

Analysis of the Act of Faith

The structure of the act of faith may be summed up briefly: while the mind is being acquainted with the Christian revelation by hearing about it from the Church, it is also interiorly illuminated by the Spirit. I need not enter into the detailed explanations of this that are given in theology. Yet I should note one point.

The scholastic account of the act of faith, according to which the intellect is strengthened to accept with certainty a doctrine which is not self-evident, is not completely satisfactory. For this is precisely the problem. How can the human mind give an absolutely certain assent to something which is devoid of compelling evidence?

After reflection it seems that the analysis should be completed. The light of faith strengthens the intellect, but it cannot give the power to act in a way which, without it, would be not only impossible but also unnatural. What then does it do? It gives the intuitive evidence that God is revealing himself, even though who he reveals himself to be is fully known only through sense-experience from the Church's teaching, preaching and life. Thus, faith results from a convergence of interior, Spirit-inspired evidence and outside acquired knowledge.

Contact with God in Faith

In faith a direct contact between God and the soul takes place. It is not enough to say that such a contact is desired; it is also achieved. Whenever we believe, we enter into immediate union with God. This contact has two aspects.

The object of faith is revelation, which is God's self-revealing to mankind in human language; God himself is therefore the object of faith. One may underline the difference between an immediate object, the proposition or formula expressing faith, and an ultimate one, God himself. Or we may simply remark that in any case God is the real object of faith since, when an action is defined according to its object, the ultimate object has primacy. The human expressions of belief are tools, not screens; they do not impede the immediacy of the believer's relation to God.

One may raise a difficulty. When, in human relationships, I believe somebody, my contact with him remains in the realm of ideas. The statement which I accept concerning him has become interior to me; but he himself remains as exterior to me as before. Our unity is not an illusion, but is not a contact between essences, for his own being is not engaged in it. In faith, however, there is the obvious difference that, whether I believe it or not, God is already interior to me by creation and by grace. Thus the object of my faith is interior to me, yet my union to him is not effected by faith but is anterior to it.

This difficulty disappears if we seek for the immediacy of faith, not in the formula of belief, but in the interior gift of light. The light of faith sparks an intuition of God which, in itself, is *clear*, though it is not *distinct* from the previous contents of the intellect and the will. Renewed in each act of faith, this intuition implies a presence of the revealing God which stays as long as faith itself. It is direct, because the light is intermediate between God and man, but is the created effect, the theological expression of the divine presence. This presence is not within the light, but given together with it.

How intimate is such a contact and what aspect of the divine reality and life does it introduce us to? We intuit God as Revealer; for he makes himself present to us in the light of faith. Revelation is done by the Three Persons together, yet it relates directly to the Word, in the humanity of Christ. The divine revelation relates the Word to mankind in general and to each man in particular through the divine humanity. The Word is intuited in faith. It is with him that we are in immediate contact.

The Father and the Holy Spirit are also contacted ("He who sees me sees the Father"), immediately because there is no creaturely intermediary, yet mediately insofar as the relation of the Word to them is the necessary way through which we reach them.

The analysis of the act of faith shows that the intellect, or faculty of knowing, is engaged in faith as the intuiting organ. Yet the seat of faith in man as receiving the light from God and as committing the whole person to him can be no other than the very center of man's being: God reveals himself at the core and the root of our personality.

Purification of Faith

The classical text on the purification of faith is *The Ascent of Mount Carmel* by St. John of the Cross. It will be the source of the following pages, although my presentation will differ. Faith is both a gift and a way of thought and life. As a gift it needs no purification, since on God's part all is perfect from the start. Yet it needs purification as a way practiced by man. What is to be purified is man's coherence with God, and since contact with God implies both recognition of the object of faith and reception of the light, purification will be twofold.

Purification in the Adhesion to Its Object

Principle: "As this is a matter wherein we must seek after and attain to God alone, God alone must be the object of our search and attainment" (*Ascent*, Bk. II, Ch. 7, v. 3).

Application: In practice, this means holding to the object of faith, as it is revealed by God, and as firmly as possible—that is:

1. Revelation should be known with the utmost clarity that we can achieve. This is not a matter of

personal research, but of obedience to the Scriptures in the Church. One will endeavor to know what the Church teaches as part of revelation without confusing with faith philosophical opinions, private revelations or personal idiosyncrasies. In the absence of such a purification, we waste some of our spiritual energy upon worthless objects; we are in danger of spiritual fatigue and disgust.

2. To adhere to faith as firmly as possible, the only way is to focus our attention upon the object of faith, eliminating from our field of attention all that is not necessary to the life of faith. One thus builds up a hierarchy with three levels: the revelation; knowledge needed to pursue our calling, which should be sought and accepted while we commit ourselves to our calling; other knowledge of a useful, aesthetic or noetic order, which should be known, while we remain unattached to it.

If this hierarchy is neglected, we waste energy over the trifles of uncentered knowledge, creating thereby more obstacles to a firm assent of faith.

Through more faithful obedience to revelation and detachment from everything else, this purification should go as far as possible toward the ideal of focusing attention on God whenever other actual knowledge is not immediately needed.

Purification in the Reception of the Light of Faith

This contact with God is far more intimate than the preceding one, being more direct. Its purification is therefore more important; and, since it implies an immediate union with God, it will have important consequences for the beginning of mystical life and the entrance into frequent contemplation. Contemplation is the experience in which man turns toward God, focusing his attention on the divine presence. Contemplation begins in the desire for God. Insofar as faith implies an immediate presence of man to God, faith is the beginning of contemplation. The purer the reception of the light of faith, the higher the contemplation.

This purification consists in focusing attention on God at the one point where his presence enlightens the soul. From this central point, this attention spreads as areas of darkness shrink. Such obstacles are attachment to other sources of lights, to points of knowledge that are of lesser value, to human authority. This purification forms the bulk of Book II in the *Ascent*. How far it should go is shown clearly by St. John of the Cross who, one after the other, eliminates not only natural acts (based upon natural lights) of sense knowledge (Bk. I) and of the mind (Bk. II, chs. 12-15), but also supernatural acts (based upon supernatural lights), like purely interior and spiritual visions (ch. 24), private revelations, even concerning God (chs. 25-27), and internal words (chs. 28-30).

The only light that St. John of the Cross admits, besides the general light of faith, is what he calls "substantial word." This is an action of God which achieves what it says. There is no difficulty as to how to discern such an intervention, since God is necessarily effective, even before the human mind is aware of his action. Consequently, the safest way to purify faith is to renounce systematically all lights that are not the light of faith, whether they come from God or not.

The sign that we are attached to a "light" which is not the *lumen fidei* is that at prayer we find solace in, and seek after, particular truths, whereas we should find peace only in a simple awareness of the presence of God in the "light of faith." This principle should of course be adjusted to our actual situation, for we may still need many truths and lights on what is not God. In any case, however, the aim should remain complete purification.

The summit of purification is reached when the soul is entirely shaped by the Spirit of God. This means a constant listening to the Word, an attention to his presence, and the adoption of a filial attitude toward the Father, in union with the one who is Son. Even before complete purification is attained, it can be temporarily anticipated and experienced with more or less intensity.

To delay such a purification means wasting energy upon misleading lights and putting obstacles to our interior progress. We should not wait for practical results in other areas to start upon it. Faith must have primacy.

II
HOPE

Hope is often considered less important than faith. We should treat them as equal, assuming that they constitute two aspects of our attitude before God, the attitude of surrender into his hands. Practically, hope is quite as important for interior progress, and its purification is just as necessary. Progress in one direction cannot be developed at the expense of other directions. All bring us to God, each according to its structure.

Analysis of the Act of Hope

1. Hope bears on a twofold object: first, future happiness with God in heaven; second, the way leading to God. Yet there is only one hope, not two, for the way is anticipated only in view of the ultimate purpose. Hence the distinction between hope and faith: faith reaches God as Truth rather than as beatifying; and between hope and despair: the object of despair is inaccessible, whereas that of hope is, by God's grace, accessible. Hence also the similarity between hope and desire (eros), the human passion directed toward happiness.

2. Since hope desires what is good, the human soul aspires to it from its capacity as *will*. It may nevertheless be distinguished from love or the gift of oneself to God. Hope consists of freely making God the purpose of our actions and taking the means to reach him by attaining to the perfection of love. It is directed to action, connected with the natural aggressivity of man. The analysis of its option for God and its expectation of his help reveals that hope implies certainty. When I hope in the eternal life, I am absolutely certain that eternal life can be reached.

3. Normally, though exceptions are frequent, this certainty follows from the practical certainty of our standing before God which originates in the self-knowledge of a good conscience. Experiencing secu-

rity in the good, the believer feels secure as to his
eternal destiny. To this basic trust, hope adds a firm
decision to seek God with one's whole strength.

4. In any case, such a certainty cannot be
reached without God's grace. God acts upon the
soul, giving certainty to its hope. Eternal happiness
and the means toward it are experienced insofar as
certainty leads to the effective orientation of the will
to God and to the introspective awareness of it.

5. There is no need to stress the fact that hope
comes from God. Its natural understructure is the
will in its function as eros, or faculty of desire; but
the act of hope derives from God's action and implies a contact with God.

As in the case of faith, this contact can be seen
from two points of view: God is "touched" both as
source and as fulfillment of hope.

Contact with God as Object of Hope

As fulfillment of hope, God is not yet touched
directly, for hope implies that we are still on the way
to him; eternal beatitude is not yet experienced,
though it is expected and desired. To say that God is
attained by hope as "ultimate concern" or purpose
of life means that hope is directed toward him in
that capacity. Yet the contact is remote. And one
may feel that a remote contact is hardly a contact.

All the same, the orientation of hope toward
God as our final end is highly important for the
inner life. For it unveils an aspect of the divine life
which would be otherwise beyond man's experience:
the munificence of God. This denotes not only the

liberality by which God creates and keeps creation, his chosen gift, but also that which he essentially is, as bearing in himself the models of all creaturely realities, which man will enjoy in the vision of God and of which he is given warrants in the providential helps and graceful aids on which hope counts. Significantly, the archetypal realities are not primary in this orientation of man toward God. Primacy belongs to the munificence of God, to the eternal movement by which God makes and sees his creation. Since all things are in the Son, the movement which gives life to all things, God's *largitas*, is no other than the divine Fatherhood, the Person of the Father. Hope places us face to face with the Father. Faith unites to the Word in a filial attitude; by hope, our life mirrors the Father's life.

Contact with God in the Certainty of Hope

God himself is the source of the certainty of hope, which is thus immediately founded upon him. It results from his presence as an almighty, munificent giver. God is thus touched as the source of our certainty, in the power and liberality of the Father. Hope implies an insight into the Father's life, which is not only noetic (source of knowledge) but existential (source of greater life for us). There is no feeling or expression of hope without this insight. Hence the possibility of centering our inner life upon the presence of the Father contacted in hope; and also the necessity of hope to understand all the implications of the presence of God.

Admittedly, we are not always reflexively conscious of our relation to the Father in our hope. But such a union with him is experienced as an existential relationship, if it is not fully conscious. Yet one may think that it is impossible to be united with God without having at least some obscure perception of it. Such a perception remains obscure as long as attention is called to other objects in which we find solace and repose. It is therefore necessary to purify hope.

The Purification of Hope

The more common doctrine is that hope is purified through a purification of memory. The reason for this is that memory keeps us attached to things, experiences and people that have been known previously. It follows that the longer we linger in past experiences through memory, the less free we are to orient our desires to the future vision of God. Thus memory may store up obstacles to a pure and steadfast orientation to the vision of God. Accordingly memory is the main subject of the purification of hope.

We can also say: hope looks forward to an object which is, relatively to us, future; whereas memory looks backward to objects that are past. Perfection demands that we overcome such a division of the self.

The process of purification of hope amounts to applying to memory what has already been said on purifying the intellect. That is, we ought not to entertain memories of experiences, physical or spiritual, that do not produce good effects in us, that is, that do not help lead us on to perfection.

Practically, the memories that ought to be entertained refer to the experiences that have had an instructive effect upon us.

Such a voiding of memory should be understood in two different ways. *At the time of prayer*, it should be as complete as possible; this is not the moment to muse about the past. *Between times of prayer*, the storing up and the use of memories we need for our practical life should go together with a spiritual unattachment to them.

In the line of thought already adopted for the certainty of hope, I would add a purification of the will which is also included in the practice of hope. Hope unites us to God insofar as God gives us to share the fruits of his self-giving. The deeper our hope, the more profound our experience of his presence—whence a lessening of concern for ventures that do not contribute to the search after the vision of God. Thus hope tends to become the chief activity of the will in its dimension as desire (eros). The sense of the presence of God deepens as we grow in hope. We become invaded by the certainty that God is our only strength.

At various times in the history of Christian spiritual doctrine, it has been suggested that the perfect Christian should place himself in the hands of God in such a way that he even abandons all expectation of ever being with God. This paradox tries to reach the highest point of abandonment of self in God. Yet three points should be maintained:

1. Hope remains always an essential constituent

of the structure of the Christian soul. Without hope, a major element in us—desire—is not being transformed into union with God.

2. Practically all orthodox mystics, even though their formulas are sometimes bold or equivocal, always teach the compatibility of hope and perfection.

3. Objections against hope rest upon the misunderstanding that hope implies a desire to appropriate God. On the contrary, it acknowledges the fact that we are destined to the vision of God and can act in order to reach it.

III
LOVE

Divine love or charity is to be explained first by reference to the human experience of love. Since "grace does not replace nature, but implies it," charity is related to human love. We experience this relationship daily. Yet the relationship is not easy to describe, and diverse accounts of it have been proposed, particularly in recent years.

An analysis of the structure of love, human and divine, may use two methods: either we analyze the human experience and psychology of love, and relate charity to it; or we analyze divine love and extend our findings to the natural structure of love. I will adopt the second method.

Hear, O Israel, the Lord our God is one Lord, and you shall love the Lord your God with all your heart and with all your soul and with all your strength. And these words which I command you shall bear upon your heart; and you shall teach them diligently to your children, and shall talk of them when you sit in your house, and when you walk by the way, and when you lie down, and when you rise. And you shall bind them as a sign upon your hands, and they shall be as frontlets between your eyes. And you shall write them on the door posts of your house and on your gates (Deut. 7:4-9).

In this passage, divine love is a total commitment:

● a sign of the Kingdom of God;
● a principle of knowledge and wisdom, guiding our vision of others and of the world;
● a principle of hospitality, that is, of the reception of the stranger as our own, which implies an identification of self with the stranger to make him our neighbor.

Divine love is therefore the love by which, being incorporated in Christ, we give our very self to God through men.

This act of love may be described psychologically and theologically. Psychologically it is a source of spiritual creativity, the upbuilding of the City of God and the development of the inner life. It has extensive social implications, since it unites man not only to God, but to all men also.

Theologically, divine love is a gift from God which lies beyond what natural man can do by himself. Given in baptism, it is inseparable from friendship with God. It already implies an anticipation of heaven.

Divine love is essentially disinterested. It is a desire for God, and therefore for union with him. Yet it is not self-centered, for it does not wish to appropriate God for man, but to give man to God. It achieves a unity through the encounter of two liberties, the liberty of God and that of man. In whatever way this self-giving may be described in detail, divine love always remains at its core the giving of self to God.

But divine love also implies love for human beings. For all men are potentially assumed in God through the Body of Christ. Every man being, in his own way, the vehicle of a presence of God, divine love strives to give man to man, i.e., man to God in man or, which amounts to the same, man to man in God, or yet, in a paradoxical formula, it gives God in man to man in God. It remains structurally the same, whether it is immediately directed toward God in himself or toward man.

The experience reaches a point where we discover that to give self to God and men is not much, if what we give is only of our own making. In the course of its development, love wishes to give what is God-like in us, the presence of God, God himself. Without ceasing to be the gift of self, it becomes a gift of God to God and to all men. For this reason it is the true bond of the family of God; it makes men all in all and all for all; it achieves union between members of the Body of Christ; it makes mankind a better image of the Trinity. In philosophical terms, love is interpersonal; it is communicative of personality, extroverting persons, and ultimately all per-

sons, in mutual spiritual intercourse. But this philo-
sophically ultimate dimension can be reached only
through God's gift, above and beyond the natural
ground of divine love.

Contact with God in Charity

The touch of God that takes place in love is
twofold: God is the object of love, and he is also its
self-giving gift.

1. *Contact with God as Object.* The case of
divine love differs from that of faith and hope, in
that the contact is more direct. For we love God as
already given to us whereas hope expects him, still
hidden, and faith believes in him, still unseen. That is
the main point of the reciprocal structure of divine
love. Not only does it tend to God; it also contacts
him because he has first given himself to us. Divine
love reaches him such as he dwells in us by grace.
This is a direct contact.

The mystical experience of God is an experience
of love, beyond thoughts and memories. For the immediacy of total union to God is granted only in
love.

2. *Contact with God as Self-Giving Gift.* Since
love implies the desire to give God to God and to
give God to all persons, it implies a contact with
God as giving himself to all who seek him. But God
giving himself is the Holy Spirit. The writings of the
mystics describe their experience of the Spirit. And
one could show it by an analysis of the exemplarity
of the Holy Spirit. Since love consists essentially in
giving God, it means that God gives himself in each

act of divine love. Man loves, and God manifests himself to the person we love. God goes out of himself and returns to himself through creation. He is immanent in our love and we are one with him when we love.

In terms of Person, it is the Holy Spirit who is directly engaged in this. He is the Archetype and the ultimate substance of all giving. In love, the touch of God brings to perfection our union to the Holy Trinity: faith touches the Son; hope touches the Father; love touches the Spirit. We are the image and the form of God's own life.

This contact with the Holy Spirit need not be conscious. Yet awareness of it is possible. The more purified is our love, the greater is our awareness of this contact. Yet even before such a purification is achieved, an obscure impression of the Holy Spirit is frequent among Christians, whether they can formulate it or not. Thus are we made God-like.

The Purification of Love

The purification of love means that we learn to be unattached to all creaturely realities, whether natural or "supernatural," whether good, evil, or indifferent.

This means that even when there is a thing or a person we love very much, we should love without being enslaved by what we love. Our inner life will grow together with a progressive renouncement of the fulfillment of our desires. The ultimate object of love must remain God; all others should be included in him. Even the good, the better, the best, or the beautiful, or the friend or the neighbor must be renounced insofar as they are outside our perception of God.

It means also that the joy and the pain which are inseparable from love should also be determined by our awareness of God. We should find joy only in God, not by stifling our sensitivity, but by educating it to be sensitive to God in all we do and in all we love. Needless to say, that is the work of a lifetime; but the advancement of the inner life is exactly proportionate to detachment for the love of God.

Perfection consists formally in love. And love is, precisely, impeded by too many loves, for the whole person cannot be engaged in divine love when it scatters its loves. Such a renunciation is not inhuman, for God contains and gives all; what we give up is transcended and recovered on a higher level. The perfect man, even in the natural level, is therefore the saint. He is the only one who perfectly enjoys all things, through a process of death and resurrection.

This purification must of course be progressive and positive. That is, trying to go too fast breeds disgust and despair, loneliness and self-delusion. While we aim at complete detachment, we should fill with God all the voids that are created in us.

The failure to start or to carry out this purification results in maiming our interior development. It may be for this reason that there are relatively few mystics. Without deciding whether mystical experience is necessary to perfection, perfection itself cannot be reached without ascetic purification. The best practical rule is never to refuse love, that is, never to refuse service.

The Moral Virtues

Many authors study the classical moral virtues, that is, the strengthening of the acts by which we build up the ethical dimension of existence, in their theoretical structure and their relative value and role. I prefer to indicate briefly their relation to faith, hope and love:

- Faith inspires, and is strengthened by, humility.
- Hope inspires, and is strengthened by, the spirit of poverty.
- Love inspires, and is strengthened by, self-denial, obedience to the needs of others, chastity or the right ordering of sex.

Others can of course be added, and other relationships could be proposed. The main point is that the ethical dimension must express the theological ground of the inner life. The progress is conditioned by a deepening of faith, hope, and love. The way to develop our ethical life is therefore to deepen our theological conviction and commitment. One can note that what Thomas Aquinas regards as the chief virtue—prudence—has a special status. Prudence is the wisdom that regulates life, measuring all that is necessary in everything we do and are. It should control all virtues and grow with them. It requires common sense and good judgment as well as spiritual discernment.

4
The Development of Prayer

The development of interior prayer is traditionally divided into three parts—purgative, illuminative, unitive—which, however, should not be considered as successive stages or phases. They are inclusive attitudes, each enfolding the others; and they are prospective, looking forward to deeper interior progress.

Many attempts have also been made to describe the successive levels reached in the course of this development. The "seven mansions" of the *Interior Castle* of St. Teresa of Avila probably constitute the most famous of these attempts.

It would be excessively artificial to keep any of these specifications because of their intrinsic value or of their standing in the tradition. While preserving their substance, I will adopt a different approach.

I

THE ETHICAL DIMENSION

The first awareness of the interior life is that which reveals to us our natural shortcomings, our ethical failures, the imperfection of our faith, hope and love, the selfishness of our relationships, in

73

short, our sinfulness. All natural tendencies are good, but they should be used according to their inherent functions and purposes; and our control of them is not always adequate. They will be brought under control:

● by the development of a healthy life which strengthens will power, and which seeks to acquire principles and methods to develop the ethical dimension of existence;

● by access to the level of interiority, through the practice of faith, hope and love, which inspires a higher practice of ascetic detachment.

I would draw attention to two important means of progress and self-control.

The concern for the good in human behavior organizes our life in view of our eternal destiny. Since it regulates action, it seeks to control all our wishes, desires, and projects, which it sets in their proper place, keeping the right proportion in all things. Essentially, it makes value judgments on the options opened to our choice and action. Its exercise depends on our spontaneous drive to know correct principles of ethical action and our courage to apply them properly. This requires knowledge, good judgment, common sense and the readiness to ask for advice. Most persons have the capacity for a good knowledge of basic moral principles and for a habitual practice of spontaneous and reflexive common sense.

The acquisition of self-control may be reduced to a development of foresight. For when foresight reigns, everything falls into place easily. The shortest way to judge the ethical dimension of action and to foresee its spiritual consequences in good or in bad is to consider it in relation to God. For the ultimate effect of a good act must tally with the purpose of God. When we know the natural structure of an act, the situation which may later affect its relation to God's design on man, and our own subjective intention as doer of the act, we are able to judge whether we can do it morally, as a step that brings us closer to God, or, on the contrary, we cannot do it without sin for it would drag us away from God.

Experience shows, however, that even "the just man" falls "seven times a day"; total avoidance of evil action is most unlikely, even for the person who is aware of being totally committed to the love of God. St. Paul expressed this movingly when he wrote: "In fact, this seems to be the rule, that every single time I want to do good, it is something evil that comes to hand. In my inmost self I dearly love God's law, but I can see that my body follows a different law that battles against the law which my reason dictates. This is what makes me a prisoner of that law of sin which lives inside my body. What a wretched man I am! Who will rescue me from this body doomed to death? Thanks be to God through Jesus Christ our Lord!" (Rom. 7:21-24).

This means that the self-knowledge needed for our interior life should include awareness of our past mistakes and patience with our present failures and shortcomings. Our attitude toward the prospect of sin should always be negative: we cannot willingly accept to commit a wrong action. But our attitude toward the memory of sin should be positive: not even my past sins can take me away from the love of God in Christ Jesus. The determination not to sin is part of our fidelity. And the acceptance of our past failures is indispensable to our patience with ourself. Patience is the acceptance of our present inacceptability. It is a necessary ingredient of our self-knowledge.

II

THE BEGINNING OF THE INTERIOR JOURNEY

From the convergence of the elements of the inner life that I have surveyed thus far, there arises the felt urgency of a life of prayer. In the usual structure of its development, this interior prayer begins with what is usually called meditation.

Meditation may be characterized by the simultaneous presence of several elements:

1. *Vocal Prayer.* This is not necessary to all prayer, but is present here in a large measure. At this stage, one needs to use words for prayer, either in spontaneous conversation with God, or by repeating some customary formula of prayer. This need of vocal prayer is perfectly natural, and may remain long after meditation has been left behind. Accordingly it is not reserved to meditation, but always is present in it.

2. *Prayer of Petition.* There are two main dimensions of prayer, petition and contemplation. Petition asks God to do something for us. It is God-centered insofar as it prays *to* him and expects to be answered by him; yet it is also self-centered insofar as the person who prays hopes to see his prayer answered. Of course, petition can be made for the sake of others; it is then hetero-centered in its purpose.

Contemplation looks at God with love, without asking for anything, whereas in meditation, petition dominates; sometimes there is nothing else. Petition can never be totally abandoned, even long after meditation has been outgrown; but its predominance characterizes meditation.

3. *Discursive Approach.* When we think about God, we may consider the mystery in itself, with no other intellectual activity than a partial intuition of its meaning. We may also attempt to reach this intellectual grasp by way of reasoning. This is done in meditation, which implies a reflexive attempt to understand something about the divine mystery. There is no meditation without reflection, for we are not yet familiar enough with the divine mysteries to contemplate them without reasoning.

All three points together form meditation.

The spiritual tradition of Christianity has known several forms of meditation. There are nonsystematic forms, or spontaneous meditations which follow no special method. These are particularly exposed to the danger of going astray and easily falling into day-dreaming. Two non-systematic forms have been widely practiced. The *lectio divina*, derived from the ancient monks, is chiefly the slow reading of a text, usually in the Bible. Reading is supplemented with our own reflections, personal applications, acts of love and petition, and resolutions. The meditated rosary consists in the vocal prayers of the rosary accompanied by reflection on the mysteries of Christ and Mary. This derives from the medieval devotion to Mary, which was more or less parallel to the meditation of the way of the Cross. Many persons simplify this and, without reference to the "mysteries," formulate the "Hail Mary" while making its meaning their own.

The systematic forms are patterns of meditation devised by spiritual writers, in order to make it easier or more efficient. These methods have been favored by some classical schools of spirituality.

All methods start from two principles:

1. Reasoning, vocal prayers and petitions are useful insofar as they help us to make acts of faith, hope, and love and to find how we ought to live according to faith, hope, and love.

2. Psychology, when it is well used, may be a powerful help in interior progress.

The classical methods are those of St. Ignatius Loyola (*Spiritual Exercises*), and of the "French School," of which there are several variants (St. Francis of Sales: *Introduction to the Devout Life*; the method of St. John Baptist de la Salle, devised for the use of the Christian Brothers). All systematically tend to deepen religious convictions by way of a constant recourse to the theological virtues, with the help of the imagination, the intellect, the sensibility, and the will. The methods vary one from another in the order in which these faculties enter into play. The differences are matters of stress rather than of essence.

III

PASSAGE TO SIMPLIFIED PRAYER

The practice of meditation develops into a well-defined direction, by progressive simplification of the three main elements of its structure.

A first simplification takes place when a special

stress is put upon some of the mental actions performed during meditation. All methods make room for elevations of the soul to God in expressions of love. This affective prayer is occupied by acts of love for God. Induced by a general view of a divine mystery, these acts of love tend to absorb all attention. They are consciously awakened by the person who wishes to make them deeper and more fervent. Some find it easy to pray in this manner. But sentimentality can be confused with fervor and natural attraction with divine love.

The simplification of interior prayer does not necessarily pass through this stage of affective prayer. The process of simplification lies within everybody's experience, when the three main structures of meditation are progressively reduced.

1. *Discursive Part.* Discursive reasoning is less and less needed before faith, hope, and love can start on their own. A greater part of prayer is now occupied by these expressions of faith, hope and love. To meditate in a methodic way may even become more or less impossible. Spontaneously, and sometimes in spite of our intention, we jump ahead of our own reflections; we anticipate their conclusion; and, taking them for granted, we leave our thought behind and simply look at God with trust. When this happens, one should not fight it; one should leave the mind alone until it is needed again.

This process is more or less slow, and there may be frequent returns to methodic meditation. The same pattern does not obtain for all. But one should recognize it for what it is: a longing after God and a desire for a simplicity patterned on the very simplicity of God.

The danger is to take sleep or absence of thought for simplification of prayer.

2. *Vocal Prayer.* The place taken by vocal prayer also changes. Short exclamations may replace the longer formulas that were helpful previously. Sometimes the same words, repeated over and over again, form a sufficient vocal background to prayer. We should not give superstitious attention to these words. What is important is our interior attitude and not its expression.

These vocal prayers also tend to be less spoken vocally than seen in the mind. The vocal organs need not function. The formula used stays in the mind as food for thought and incentive to love.

3. *Petition.* Although petition never disappears, one comes to find more solace in a more contemplative prayer. We look at God in faith; we would like to remain in his presence forever; we seek no particular grace, but we implore God in a general way to keep us attached to him. In this substitution of contemplation for petition, we run the danger of selfishness. For simplification is satisfying. We feel satisfied, for simplification fits our current needs. Accordingly, we are inclined to value this feeling of satisfaction and long for it, thus substituting a personal pleasure for God. The way to counterbalance this selfishness is provided by the purification of faith.

The growing difficulty to meditate may surprise us, be interpreted as a result of some hidden sin, and foster despondency and worry. We should then remember that despondency and worry never come from God. And we should seek for advice from a competent counselor.

IV
DEEPENING OF SIMPLIFIED PRAYER

The deepening of simplified prayer is one of the most important phases in the development of interior life. After meditation is outgrown, simplified prayer itself deepens and grows. This development takes two directions.

In Extension. The general impression of the presence of God tends to remain even if we do not apply our attention to it. As a background to what we do, a silent adoration goes on in our soul. Everything we do is influenced by it. The importance of silence at this period of spiritual life cannot be overstressed. It staves off intrusions upon our awareness of God.

In Intensity. Interior prayer develops also in intensity. The main characteristics of this development will be listed in an order of growing importance.

Concerning Sensibility. Until now many distractions in prayer were caused by interferences from our sensations: cold or heat affect us, noise disturbs us and causes many wanderings of the mind. This now tends to diminish. Sounds and things still interfere with us, but our attention is led away less and less. This is not due to conscious efforts on our part but it seems to come about easily.

Concerning Imagination. Hitherto many distractions were caused by mental images of all kinds. This happens constantly in our life but it is a special nuisance when we wish to concentrate on religious matters. It does not cease in the development of simplified prayer, but it is no longer a cause of distraction. Our mental activity now goes on two planes: that of imagination, which creates and moves images largely beyond our control; and that of faith, love and hope. These planes do not meet, so that mental images need not interfere with love, hope, and faith. They interfere only when our activity is not sufficiently theocentric. Now we are still praying —and perhaps very deeply—in spite of what at other times would be distracting. These two levels should be distinguished very clearly, so that we may follow as fully as possible faith, love and hope.

Concerning the Will. The attitude of our will is then one of praise and love of God. We offer ourselves to God for any purpose he may have. If this self-offering is accompanied by the purification of the will, this is a sign that we are effectively progressing toward God. It requires, obviously, that we deeply desire God's will and that we wish to love all men fraternally. Desiring to know and to do God's will, we seek for it in the presence of God among men. Prayer inspires a life of obedience. This may still co-exist with sins and bad habits, which cannot be given up all at once. But the desire to uproot them is strong, even if we still experience many hesitancies at the extent of the generosity and self-abnegation that may be asked of us.

Concerning the Intellect. The intellectual aspect of the simplification of prayer is more complex. Usually, prayer now starts with a general view of some aspect of the Christian mystery. Yet attention is focused less on the particularity of the mystery than on the universality of God-in-Christ. All mysteries express God's presence in Christ. We therefore seek God in Christ in a general way. Reflection may still play some part, but the tendency is to replace it by a quiet attention to God in faith. Attention does not pass from subject to subject or even from one to another aspect of the same subject; we are aware of the presence of God and we entrust ourselves to it. The basic attitude of faith and hope becomes more and more encompassing.

First Mystical Graces

During this development, we may receive graces which strengthen our perseverance in prayer. These graces seem to be of three kinds:

1. *A Transitory Absorption in Prayer*. While we are intent upon loving God, believing him and hoping in him, consciousness of the surrounding world is suddenly dimmed; there seem to be only God and myself; and it is with surprise that our familiar surroundings re-enter our stream of consciousness. This is explained by the intensity of our acts of faith and of love, which may exclude all else from consciousness. Sense-perception continues, yet without reaching the level of awareness.

The danger here is that a purely psychological kind of self-absorption may be mistaken for this. We may so concentrate on excluding distractions that the focal point of our attention is not the presence of God, but the void within us. It is quite possible, even without any reference to the spiritual dimension, to remain so absorbed in the center of the self that we are aware of nothing else.

2. *Spiritual Joy*. Our consciousness may be invaded by impressions of spiritual comfort. The friendship of God that we experience may be accom-

panied by an impression of the goodness of God, which we cannot resist. These impressions may persist and may last several days. What has happened is simple: the grace strengthening our love for God has let its effect overflow so that these have been felt indirectly in the sensitive part of the psyche, thus creating an impression of spiritual joy.

The danger lies in becoming attached to this, which would not be compatible with the full purification of our love. The advice traditionally given is therefore never to seek such graces and, when they come, simply to let them pass and to seek God alone all the more.

3. *Sudden Strong Desires of Serving God Better.* These come all of a sudden and seem to carry us rather than to proceed from our initiative. Their impact and the love which they foster may far exceed our usual level of commitment. Even when these aspirations disappear, they leave their mark, in the form, for instance, of more love and generosity.

They need to be controlled, for we can easily misinterpret our generosity. This must be oriented toward more effective love rather than toward forms of asceticism, which would not necessarily correspond to, or help develop, love. Ascetic self-control may be no more than a reaction of compensation for the grace we have received. It is true that a wish to do penance may translate a deep view of the function of Jesus crucified and a longing after union with him. Yet the risk of confusion with masochistic tendencies should be taken into account.

The development of simplified prayer forms a very important phase of the inner life. Yet the levels that are reached in it still remain relatively inferior.

The graces and insights received are meant to help our growth and are by no means signs of personal holiness. God calls us nearer to himself. His interventions require our active collaboration, when the sudden light of their reception is past. And if such a collaboration is not given, we may well relapse to more superficial levels of interiority. These insights are compatible with the usual lapses into sinfulness that even holy persons cannot escape. They help to discern these and to overcome them.

V
THE PASSAGE TO CONTEMPLATION

This phase may be seen from the point of view of theory: What happens when the soul enters contemplation? Or, from that of practice: Are there signs that one is entering mystical life? The answer to the second question should lead us to answering the first.

At this point I will simply recall the doctrine of St. John of the Cross on the three signs of entrance to contemplation (*Ascent*, Bk. II, ch. 14-15). When a soul is entering mystical life, three signs are found *simultaneously:*

1. She is unable to meditate discursively and to make use of her imagination in prayer. This implies that previously she did use her imagination and was able to meditate. Then, either all at once or progressively, this becomes impossible. Obviously, a temporary incapacity may derive from fatigue or from frequent distractions in prayer. When this appears without the other signs, it should be attributed to a

natural cause, physical or psychological, which should be investigated and removed.

2. She finds unattractive or even repulsive the consideration by her mind of all that is not God. This negative sign would not suffice by itself, for it could derive from nervousness or tiredness.

3. She finds joy at being alone with God, at looking at him quietly in a general way; she has peace whenever she so looks at him. Her mind and imagination no longer interfere with that silent prayer. Her attitude of love and adoration is not focused on any particular aspect of God, but on God in himself without secondary qualifications. This sign cannot be due to physical or psychological causes, and is therefore the main one. However, if it is not accompanied by the first two, it is not effectively there, and we are mistaken or deluded about its presence.

What has now happened is that mystical graces have become more permanent. As we become accustomed to them, they do not seem so sudden as before; but being more permanent, they render previous ways of prayer impossible. This may be a source of suffering. For, if the passage has been fast, we may still naturally hanker after our former habits of reflection and meditation. Their loss leaves us bewildered. Thus it may happen that we strain our mind trying to meditate, whereas we ought simply to accept silently what God is doing in us. The attitude to adopt during this passage is one of simple and general adhesion to God. To all appearances his ways are out of the ordinary and leave us somewhat puzzled; but he knows what he is doing. Faith, hope, and love should quietly follow the path traced by

God. To go back to the ways we prefer would be a mistake with the painful consequence of attempting the impossible and thus courting the danger of despair.

If we are called on to give advice to a person who is in this transition we should beware of substituting our own methods for the ways of God. To impose on someone an attitude which does not correspond with the actual action of God would be a serious misdirection. It may be due to this that some, perhaps many, do not go beyond this stage of their interior journey.

VI
CONTEMPLATION

We now place ourselves in the hypothesis of a person who has passed the difficult entrance into contemplation.

Nature of Contemplation

This may be described in two ways, according to two standpoints. Contemplation may be viewed theologically as the fruition of sanctifying grace. It is an objective transformation of the soul which, under the influence of the Holy Spirit, is made to act passively. The standpoint of experience, favored by Carmelite authors, starts from the testimonies of the mystics who describe what they have experienced. Contemplation is then the subjective consciousness of a special action of God in us. Thus we may stress the inner transformation or the awareness of it, with the possible danger of understressing the other aspect.

The doctrine of St. John of the Cross builds a bridge between these two approaches. It happens in the development of the inner life that we experience "substantial words," that is, words which do not come from our own activity, but are completely formed in us all of a sudden and are efficacious by themselves. "Substantial words produce vivid and substantial effects upon the soul. . . . Only such a word is substantial as impresses substantially on the soul that which it signifies. It is as if Our Lord were to say formally to the soul: 'Be thou good'; it would then substantially be good" (*Ascent*, II, ch. 31, n. 1). This is called a "word," because it is, as it were, heard; it implies consciousness. It is qualified as "substantial" because it affects the interior substance of man, his central reality, which it transforms for the better. The two aspects of "inner transformation" and of "consciousness" are joined here.

It is true that St. John of the Cross does not define contemplation as a "substantial word." Yet, for him, "substantial words" constitute the only kind of special knowledge which is not to be left behind in the thrust of contemplation: one "should neither desire them nor refrain from desiring them" (*idem*, n. 2). For although they are not God, they come from him. Thus they initiate to a contemplative experience. And their two chief characteristics subsist in all mystical contemplation.

The first is *consciousness*. A more or less vivid impression is given of something passively received from God. Such a consciousness is not discursive knowledge, but an experiential awareness, similar to the knowledge a person has of himself. Without this consciousness, the mystical experience could not be described.

The second is *effective transformation*. The grace of contemplation is self-sufficient in achieving what it signifies, and this is no other than our union with God. The "substantial" reality underlying it is the coming of God himself acting within us, as a result of which we are passively transformed. God himself comes to us. Yet we may say that what we experience is only a development of the life of faith, where God is already present. The feeling of this presence is intensified: grace is the inchoateness of glory. Whether we explain this intensification with reference to the theology of the gifts of the Holy Spirit (St. Thomas) or that of the beatitudes (St. Bonaventure), or in any other possible way, makes little difference. The main point remains: it is the work of God himself.

Mystical contemplation differs in kind from the development of simplified prayer. Simplification is ruled largely by psychological law and depends to a great extent on progressive and intelligent efforts. Contemplation comes only from a free choice of God that cannot be resisted by man. God invades our consciousness, and we know him when he is already there. This is called "passivity."

Should one desire contemplation? We saw, in explaining the purification of love, that nothing but God should be desired ultimately. It seems clear, therefore, that contemplation, being the intense presence of God in us, may be desired. But the answer to the question "should it?" depends upon a previous theological opinion on the nature of contemplation. If, as some hold it, contemplation is the normal outcome of Christian life, then it should be desired, just as perfection, of which it is then an aspect. If, as others think, mystical contemplation is only one among many paths to perfection, it should be desired conditionally, that is, provided that it corresponds to our personal vocation.

Trinitarian Structure

At its summit, mystical experience is a discovery of, and a participation in, the Trinity. The testimonies of the Catholic mystics are unanimous on this point, even though their descriptions differ. It is a discovery of the relations of the Word with the Father and with the Spirit, by way of our own participation in the divine sonship of the Word. Communion with the Word of God "is a commerce of spirit to Spirit and of spirit in Spirit," in which the life of the Spirit is experienced in its three personal manifestations: Word, Spirit, Father.

This implies that all the inner life is a progressive revelation, in our experience, of the Three Persons. It consists in "going to God the Father, through the Son, in the Holy Spirit."

Going to God the Father. This is the ultimate, and our life should converge upon the ultimate. By learning about the Father, we place ourselves in a position where we may know, no longer only about him, but him, where he shows himself to us. Learning about him is not only or mainly a matter of objective study; it is first a matter of subjectively taking the interior attitude and adopting the exterior behavior of a child of God. This is the truth reached by St. Thérèse of Lisieux with her "little way." We can learn the greatness of God by practicing our own littleness, which is only the counterpart of it. God reveals himself to little ones. Thus, humility is the ascetic translation of the mystical discovery of God as Abyss. The abyss calls to the Abyss: the abyss of nothingness to the Abyss of Being. The attributes of God (goodness, immensity, almightiness, etc.) are not so much analogical transferences of human qualities, by way of "eminence," as rather anagogical (mystical) opposites of human lacks and shortcomings that are perceived by way of a "negation" applied to our lacks and shortcomings. The immanence and the transcendence of God appear, not as balancing attributes, but as amazing condescensions of God, who hides his immanence in our impermanence and reflects his transcendence in our contingency.

Through the Son. It is impossible to be filial in relation to the Father without the mediation of the eternal Son, for only in him are we also children of God. Outside of him, we remain aliens. Through him, we are associated to his filiation. The ultimate purpose of the Incarnation is to make his sonship known to us and to enable us to participate in it through our sharing in his human nature. The human nature of Christ is our channel to God. Our union to Christ must pass from his humanity to his divinity. From his human spirit, as revealed in Scripture, we must learn about his divine Spirit; and from this we must learn his divine Spirit as he communicates himself to us. The means of this passage is the liturgical and sacramental life, which, under the impact of mystical prayer, we understand more and more according to the spirit. The Church itself belongs to this sacramental order, which must be shared, not according to the letter, but according to the spirit. There is a dialectic and mutual implication of the visible and the invisible, the symbol and its meaning, the Church on earth and the Kingdom in heaven. To go to the Father *through the Son* means to be rooted in the mediation of the Son, which is expressed through the Incarnation and made present to us through the very earthiness and institutionality of the community.

In the Holy Spirit. Without the Spirit, we cannot understand the Son according to the Spirit, but only according to the flesh. We should therefore let ourselves be led by the Spirit. This implies docility to his love when it is manifested to us, and desire to know it when it is not. It implies freedom, for "where the Spirit of God is, there is freedom," that is, not freedom *from* anything, but freedom *to* follow the always unexpected guidance of the Spirit. The Spirit of freedom is also a Spirit of fellowship, for instead of dividing, like the spirit of man, he unites. Spiritual freedom is a source of unity, when we recognize the Spirit in each and all. Far from taking us away from men, the interior journey brings us to them. We encounter God in solitude, face to face, but this encounter comes to fruition in commitment to those in whom also the Spirit is present. Thus the encounter of the Three Persons forms the summit and the sum total of the inner life. The mystical grace of knowledge and love through experience crowns a previous attitude of unity with the Son in the inspirations of his Spirit leading us to the Ground and Abyss of Being, God the Father.

Conclusion

The records of the highest mystical experiences left by the Christian mystics show that these may be divided into mystics of light and mystics of darkness. Some express their highest experiences in terms of light and fulfillment, others in terms of night, void, cloud, abyss. Some see the Three Persons exploding out of the unity of God; others see the unity of God absorbing the Three Persons in its abyss. The two phases may alternate in the same writings. They seem to refer to two aspects of God, the knowable and the unknowable. Even at the acme of mystical union, God remains unknowable, and the ultimate aspect of God is always his inaccessibility.

The various ways the mystics speak of this are partly the outcome of differing spiritual paths and experiences, partly a matter of literary translation and theological explanation, by them, of their ineffable experience.

All along spiritual life, God may be known also in these two ways, as light, presence, ground of our being, fulfillment, spouse; or as night, darkness, absence, cloud, abyss of all being, the inaccessible, the all-other. Some spiritual tempers are better attuned to perceive the immanence, others the transcendence, of God. The way of immanence usually leads to an illuminated knowledge and awareness of God, the way of transcendence to an obscure awareness of him in the night. But the two may also alternate in everyday experience. And the obscure knowledge of God as absent may well be better than the joyful knowledge of him as present, for it is less liable to illusion and misinterpretation.

The state which I now experience . . . is an altogether extraordinary clarity in the ways of the super-adorable Spirit of the Incarnate Word, whom I experience, in great purity and certainty, to be objective Love, intimately united and uniting my spirit to his, and that everything he has said is spirit and life in me (Venerable Mary of the Incarnation: *Relation of 1654*, n. LXVII).

Conclusion

In an address on December 27, 1972, Pope Paul VI accurately described the situation of modern man, who is so busy with a variety of tasks that he lives outside of himself:

We are usually absorbed in exterior concerns. Our thoughts, our actions, are extrovert. We do not take time to think about ourselves; I mean that we cannot ponder, create a little silence, a little solitude, a little quiet in ourselves. Even when our actions have a personal character, when we think, read, study, our attention goes beyond the act of self-awareness. This is well known, and it is even willed. The program of our life is characterized by intensive external activities which, through an exhausting rhythm of work, impose set cadences upon our times, so that, as soon as we have a moment, an hour, a day at our disposal, we need distraction; at another rhythm and with other concerns we escape our interior upper room, our inner conversation, where perhaps we would like to linger, but we are afraid of being alone, afraid of discovering the vanity of things.

In an age of hyper-activity like ours, Christians are

tempted to follow the easy way, to pass from the programmed gestures of their working day to the packaged distractions of popular culture made available to every home by television.

Such a situation clashes with the Christian conception of the purpose of existence and the meaning of life. We are not created for business, but for God. Whether it is oriented toward acquisition of the good things of life for the purpose of reaching human happiness (as usually conceived in the context of American life) or it is primarily geared toward the transformation of the world with the purpose of creating an ideal society in the future (as usually conceived in Communist countries), today's urge to be always doing something draws man away from what religion has always identified as the aim of life, namely, the contemplation of God. In a Christian context, action is a means to a higher end. The believer should never be so totally absorbed in action as to lack the leisure or the inclination to consider that to which action tends: the vision of the divine beauty. For this reason the Old Testament prescribed that the toil of the week should prepare the peace of the Sabbath, and the Christian tradition has seen Sunday as a day of rest, that is, a day of prayerful, contemplative leisure.

Yet one should distinguish between different types of contemplation. Aesthetic absorption in the world runs the danger of dissipation in the multiplicity of things. Contemplation of oneself in the inner recesses of our being, which is made fashionable by the "drug culture" of our day, would ultimately bring us face to face with emptiness within us. Both the world outside and the self inside must themselves be means to find the Absolute. They constitute the "ladder of creatures" up which the saints of the Catholic tradition have been raised toward the living God. The purpose of life is the contemplation of God. And as God is himself living, this implies participation in his life: in the Spirit we are led, through the Son, to the Father. Pope Paul himself has reminded us that the Church originates in the descent of the Spirit. Commenting on Pentecost (May 17, 1972), he has said:

> This was the Holy Spirit, that is, the living Love, Third Person of the Holy Trinity, God himself proceeding from God the Father and God the Son, who is the Word. The one God thus revealed himself in the mystery of his inner, infinite, unfathomable life, made accessible to men in a certain manner, in a way which remains minute and analogical before the infinite reality of God, One in Three Persons, but overflowing with light, joy and mystery for the spirit of the man who has been filled with it.

But, as the Pope added, "in order to grasp the supernatural waves of the Spirit, a rule, a requirement naturally imposes itself: the inner life. It is within the soul that encounter takes place with this ineffable guest."

What are the conditions of the inner life, if it is to lead us to contemplating God in the power of the Spirit? Since it is offered to all in the Church and all are called to it, contemplation is grounded in the ordinary graces given to us by God day by day. The *constitutive elements* of the Spirit-oriented inner life are no other than the natural capacities of man, implanted in him by the Creator, as, healed from the wounds of sin by baptism and faith, they are also strengthened and transformed. This healing and this transformation are progressively effected by assiduous and faithful reception of the sacraments of faith, by participation in worship, by meditative reading of the Scriptures, by the development of personal prayer. These constitutive elements of the inner life contribute to growth toward the perfection of the Beatitudes ("Blessed are the pure in heart, for they shall see God"—Mt. 5:8) through the impact of *dynamic principles* by which the divine grace guides us through faith, hope and love toward the ascent to God along the degrees of prayer. All through this pilgrimage, the Christian is led by trust in the promise of Christ: "If anyone loves me, he will keep my word, and my Father will love him, and we shall come to him, and make our dwelling with him" (Jn. 14:23).

The search for God above us in the transcendence of his Trinitarian life necessarily passes through the encounter of God within us. Having entered into ourselves, when all creatures are silenced, we may hear the wonderful silence of the hidden God who attracts us to himself. The *development of prayer* coincides with the map of this interior journey toward "the Father of light" from whom "all that is good, everything that is perfect, is given us from above" (Jas. 1:16-17). Because he is also "the Father of our Lord Jesus Christ" (Eph. 1:3), this journey to the Father requires that we share in the sonship of the Eternal Son, and follow the example of his earthly life. Jesus is the perennial model and the only mediator of Christian sanctification and contemplation. And as Jesus left the Church upon earth as the community of the saints united in him, it is only in fidelity to the Church that we can have access to the Father. The verticality of divine grace includes the horizontality of communion with one another, expressed in human brotherhood at the service of the Gospel. In this perspective, one cannot legitimately oppose the Church and the individual, the institution and personal fulfillment, the outside and the inside. Indeed, the Church is inseparably both. In the words of Vatican Council II, she is "at the same time human and divine, visible and endowed with invisible qualities, fervent in action and absorbed in contemplation, present in the world and on pilgrimage" (*Constitution on the Sacred Liturgy*, n. 2).

It is in order to help more Christians to find their way back, out of the agitation of modern times, to the simplicity of man's encounter with the Lord that the present volume has been written. For, as the Council has also reminded us:

> To each and every one of his followers, no matter what their place in life, the Lord Jesus, divine master and model of all perfection, preached the holiness of life of which he himself is the author and the perfecter: "You, therefore, are to be perfect as your heavenly Father is perfect" (Mt. 5:48). . . . Hence, it should be perfectly clear to everyone that all the Christian faithful of whatever rank or condition are called to the fullness of Christian life and to the perfection of charity (*Constitution on the Church*, n. 40).

Bibliography

CHAPTER 1: INTRODUCTION

Thomas Merton: *The Ascent to Truth*, New York, 1951; Pierre Pourrat: *Christian Spirituality*, Westminster, Md., 1953; Pierre Teilhard de Chardin: *The Divine Milieu*, New York, 1960; Bruno Scott James: *Seeking God*, New York, 1960; Hans Urs Von Balthasar: *Prayer*, New York, 1961; Hilda Graef: *The Story of Mysticism*, New York, 1965; Paul Evdokimov: *The Struggle with God*, New York, 1966; Alfons Auer: *Open to the World: An Analysis of Lay Spirituality*, Baltimore, 1966; Michel Quoist: *The Christian Response*, New York, 1967; Louis Evely: *The Prayer of a Modern Man*, Wilkes-Barre, Pa., 1968; Edward Carter: *Response in Christ: A Study of the Christian Life*, Dayton, 1969; William Doty: *Holiness for All: Vatican II Spirituality*, St. Louis, 1969.

CHAPTER 2: CONSTITUTIVE ELEMENTS

On World Religions: Sidney Spencer: *Mysticism in World Religions*, London, 1963; Aelred Graham: *Zen Catholicism*, London, 1964; *Conversations*,

Christian and Buddhist, New York, 1968; Thomas Merton: *Mystics and Zen Masters*, New York, 1967; John Dunne: *The Way of All the Earth*, New York, 1972; J.M. Déchanet: *Christian Yoga*, New York, 1972.

On the Human Situation: Pierre Teilhard de Chardin: *The Phenomenon of Man*, New York, 1959; John Dunne: *The City of the Gods*, New York, 1965; Ralph Harper: *Nostalgia*, Cleveland, 1966; Miguel de Unamuno: *The Tragic Sense of Life*, Princeton, 1973.

On the Sacraments: Louis Bouyer: *Liturgical Piety*, Notre Dame, 1955; *Introduction to Spirituality*, New York, 1961; *Rite and Man*, Notre Dame, 1963; *Eucharist*, Notre Dame, 1968; Thomas Merton: *Life and Holiness*, New York, 1963; Eugene Cuskelly: *A Heart To Know Thee. A Practical Summa of the Spiritual Life*, Westminster, Md., 1965; Alexander Schmemann: *Sacraments and Orthodoxy*, New York, 1965.

On Prayer: William McNamara: *The Art of Being Human*, Milwaukee, 1962; *The Human Adventure: Contemplation for Everyman*, New York, 1974; François Durrwell: *In the Redeeming Christ: Toward a Theology of Spirituality*, New York, 1963; Michel Quoist: *Prayers*, New York, 1963; Douglas Steere: *Dimensions of Prayer*, New York, 1963; René Voillaume: *Seeds of the Desert*, Notre Dame, 1964; *Brothers of Men*, Baltimore, 1966; Alan Paton: *Instrument of Thy Peace*, New York, 1968; George Tavard: *Meditation on the Word*, New

York, 1969; Louis Evely: *Our Prayer*, New York, 1970; Edward O'Connor: *The Pentecostal Movement in the Catholic Church*, Notre Dame, 1971.

CHAPTER 3: DYNAMIC PRINCIPLES

Bernard Lonergan: *Insight*, New York, 1957; Jacques Maritain: *The Degrees of Knowledge*, New York, 1959; Martin Thornton: *English Spirituality: An Outline of Ascetical Theology According to the English Pastoral Tradition*, London, 1963; Thomas Merton: *Contemplative Prayer*, New York, 1969; Thomas Gannon and George Traub: *The Desert and the City: An Interpretation of the History of Spirituality*, New York, 1969; Michel Quoist: *Christ Is Alive*, New York, 1971; *I've Met Jesus Christ*, New York, 1973.

Several classics should be read at this point: Nicholas of Cusa: *The Vision of God*, New York, 1960; St. John of the Cross: *The Ascent of Mount Carmel* (*Collected Works*, tr. by K. Kavanaugh and O. Rodriguez, New York, 1964); William Law: *A Serious Call to a Devout and Holy Life*, Edinburgh, 1961; Thomas Traherne: *The Centuries*, London, 1963.

CHAPTER 4: DEVELOPMENT OF PRAYER

One should read chiefly here some of the classics, such as: St. Bonaventure: *The Mind's Road to God*, New York, 1953; Anonymous: *The Cloud of Unknowing*, London, 1971; St. Teresa of Avila: *Auto-*

biography, New York, 1960; St. John of the Cross: *The Spiritual Canticle*; Anonymous: *The Way of a Pilgrim*, New York, 1965; William of St. Thierry: *The Golden Epistle*, Spencer, Mass., 1971.